THE 1° SHIFT

DISCOVER THE SIMPLICITY OF LASTING CHANGE

FLORA SAGE

First Edition: January 2021

For information contact:

Flora Sage

www.florasage.com

flora@florasage.com

ISBN 978-1-7357503-0-9 (paperback)

ISBN 978-1-7357503-1-6 (ebook)

Published by Daves WRC

www.daveswrc.com

For my sons, Gage and Chase, the two men I have been so fortunate to raise and watch become the most resilient and incredible individuals I have ever known.

You both inspire me daily and will continue to be my greatest teachers.

CONTENTS

APPENDIX

ACKNOWLEDGMENTS

This book, like everything else I have created, has been the result of a huge team effort. I want to express my deepest gratitude and thanks to:

Katrina Ruth, fellow business coach and mentor. I am so grateful that, during a time when my steps forward were clouded and I could truly only see the next step before me, our conversation early one morning finally pushed me to write this book. Thank you so very much.

Heather Monahan, speaker and fellow coach. Thank you for being such an incredibly clear voice for this work and showing me how my message can truly change the course of my life and work forever.

Ryan Dempsey, fellow writer and thinker. Thank you for helping to nurture the seed of this book to help it see the light of day.

Laura and Stephen Gardner, my right and left hand at Flora Sage International. You both are truly an answer to my prayers. Thank you for your belief in me, my work, the vision held for this book, and the impact we know it's making on the planet. I may have founded the company, but because it is fully supported by your brilliance and dedication, we are going to impact millions of lives.

Emily Daves, my developmental editor and team. Thank you for your extraordinary talents, attention to detail, and word-smithing magic—this book is truly a gift from above. Thank you for your endless hours of meetings, texts, emails, proofing, and rewrites to make this work all that it could be.

Andrea Crowder fellow coach, light worker, and change-maker. I am grateful for our brief, yet powerful conversations and your coaching. They remind me each time to listen even more intently to my inner knowing and to ignore the chatter around me. Thank you for never dimming your light and being the badass that you are.

To all my current and past clients that I've had over the years. Thank you for helping me refine the 1° Shift Method through our coaching sessions and classes. Thank you for applying what I've taught you and for showing me the magnitude that this process can have in your lives.

To all the beta and proofreaders. Thank you for your valuable input and insights. This book is better because of you.

Finally, to my partner in life, Kenneth Alan! You are my rock. I am so grateful to have someone like you in my life. Thank you for believing in me when so many didn't. Thank you for seeing my vision and knowing it was not a pipe dream but a clear vision of where I was headed.

INTRODUCTION

Imagine this: You're sixteen years old. You walk into the house after school to see your Dad standing by the patio door, holding a scotch and water with a solemn look on his face.

Scotch and water meant one of two things when it came to my dad: there was a party or a problem. Let's just say that there were no balloons in sight.

I knew everything was about to change.

He looked away from me and said, "Kid, I'm sorry. She said it's either you or her. You have to go."

My stepmother wanted me out of the house permanently. She was never very fond of me or my sisters. It was all the proof I needed in three scotch-stained sentences.

The next half hour was a blur as I crammed everything I could into my 1989 Chevy Celebrity and drove to my best friend Jenny's house. She was waiting at the curb when I arrived.

She hugged me until the tears stopped flowing. The last time we hugged like that was four years earlier at my mother's funeral. My mom died in a car accident, leaving my dad to father five girls on his own. We were 19, 18, 15, 13, and 12 at the time. I was the baby of the family.

A year and a half later, I was just stepping into adolescence, missing my mom more than ever—and my dad was getting re-married. My stepmom had two daughters, which brought the grand total to seven girls, and unfortunately, my new mom-to-be was more a fan of the bottle than having five new daughters.

Things quickly spiraled out of control. I found myself being the scapegoat for everything wrong in their marriage and every-thing wrong in the house. If my sisters didn't do their chores, I would be punished. When the house was a mess, I had to clean it up. Many of my nights were spent locked in my room without access to a bathroom or food—only for her to not remember any of it the next morning. I would come out of my room to empty my trash can of bathroom waste from the night before, only to have her give me a chipper "good morning" over her morning coffee.

Soon I began partying and staying out as much as possible to avoid what was waiting for me at home. Once I turned 16, I bought a car that gave me even greater access to parties, one-night stands, and every avenue I could find to numb all that I was feeling (or trying not to feel). Losing my mom was hard enough, but when my Dad remarried, I felt like I'd lost him too.

After moving out and into an apartment that I shared with one of my older sisters and two of her classmates, I started a full-time job and barely graduated high school with a GPA of 1.95. At 17 years old, all I knew was that I wanted out. My "out" was the Marine Corps. I had no idea what I was getting myself into, but anything was better than what I was stepping out from.

I graduated from boot camp on my 18th birthday, and I'd like to tell you that things have been roses ever since, but honestly, that's far from the truth. I spent the better part of my life being tossed about by the waves of uncertainty, being afraid of change, being frozen in a negative mindset, and drowning in my own bullshit. And then, one day, everything changed. I'd hit rock bottom and decided that I was done living a direction-less life. I found a scrap of a vision and began resetting my habits. I confronted my bullshit, honed that vision, and began shifting my life toward all that was possible. I changed every-thing. I did it step-by-step, day-by-day, and one degree at a time.

Now I'm living my dream. I live in a beautiful home, my kids are grown and healthy, my business is booming, my life partner is incredible, and we have a fabulous dog that keeps us all entertained. I've designed the life I've always wanted and created days that are mostly stress-free. The 1° Shift is a life-style I continue to implement, and it's the secret to my success —my financial success, my relational success, my emotional success, and my spiritual success—and it can be yours too. The clarity, confidence, and courage you need to change your life are well within your reach.

I invite you to believe in the simplicity of lasting change. Your dream life awaits. Your time is now.

PART I
THE SHIFT

EVERYONE IS LOOKING

"Not how long, but how well you lived is the main thing."
~ Seneca

*E*veryone is looking for something, that secret strategy to get what they want—that next game-changer. Everyone wants whatever *that* is. I grew up expecting life to be a series of grand, epic events that shape us to the core. What I really needed was not a grand event but a shift. A shift in perspective, a shift in income, a shift in relationships—the list goes on and on.

Due to this desire, we often find ourselves chasing happiness—chasing things that promise the gold at the end of the rainbow. The *idea* of "happiness" can manifest itself in many ways. This looks like signing up for a class after a class in hopes another certification will matter. Starting yet another diet in hopes of fitting into those smaller jeans. Ending and starting new relationships, only to have the same problems repeat themselves, no matter who we are with.

Sometimes, we can feel like the problems in our lives are chasing us. When this happens, we go numb or step into avoidance behaviors. We don't want to deal with things that are "too much." Bad relationships, overeating, overspending, a job we hate, things not working out the way we want, the way we desire, the way we need. The list goes on and on, and yes, there's a reason binging on Netflix is a thing. We do things to distract ourselves from dealing with what's really going on… to keep from dealing with the elephant in the room. This also looks like over-committing, volunteering too often, getting involved in too many "hobbies" so that we are constantly doing *something*. The reality is, working overtime or staying late at the office might just be more about retreating than pursuit.

Chasing happiness and running from whatever is chasing us are both ways that we subconsciously scream out that we are ready for a shift—that we are ready for change. Everyone is seeking one thing that will solve all their problems. We are all seeking that life-changing event that will shift everything all at once.

The truth is, the things that lead us to what we're searching for —the things that give us those core-shaping moments—are not found in one grand event but in tiny little wisps of singular moments. It's the subtle and seemingly benign moments that string together a life that can and will shape who we are. If we don't pay attention, we will miss those moments *and* the beauty within them.

So, what happens when we begin to pay attention and look for those tiny moments in our lives?

Magic! Pure magic.

It is in the recognition and pursuit of the tiniest of moments that our lives can shift from where we are to where we ultimately desire to be. The epic events do exist—just not in the way we expect. Instead, they manifest through focused intention on individual moments.

1°

There is a way to find what you're looking for within those tiny moments.

Years ago, I was taking a class from Bob Proctor, an amazing mentor of mine, and during this class, he offered a great metaphor. He said, if you have a car on a single lane going from the East Coast to the West Coast, and you set the navigation to go straight, you will go in a straight line to your destination. However, if you change the trajectory just 1/16 of an inch to the right or left, you could end up in Canada or Mexico by the time you reach the coast. Just one slight, almost unrecognizable change to your path can drastically change your destination and your life over time.

Another example that depicts this well is represented in James Clear's book, *Atomic Habits*. In the book, he talks about the British cycling team and how they never won a Tour de France race in over 110 years, until one day when the team hired a new performance director who established a goal of improving the cycling team by 1%. Not as a team overall but in various areas of performance, on and off the course.

His philosophy: "The whole principle came from the idea that if you broke down everything you could think of that goes into riding a bike, and then improve it by 1%, you will get a significant increase when you put them all together."

They began making tiny adjustments in their bike seats, changing the type of tires they used, the type of massage gels they used after practice, the types of pillows and mattresses they slept on etc. Utilizing this strategy, British cyclists went from zero wins to 178 world championships and 66 Olympic or Paralympic gold medals. Additionally, they captured five Tour de France victories. All of this came to fruition from noticing those tiny components that could be improved upon in singular ways—and acting on them.

THE 1° SHIFT

The above examples are just two of many that represent the concept of the 1° Shift. This concept is the secret to creating lasting change—that works. Yeah, change is hard. It's ugly, scary, and frankly, it sucks. So, how can we create lasting change that doesn't feel like we're getting a root canal? By doing it 1° at a time.

If you've had trouble with change, it's not your fault. Most people think change is a full swing—a 180° shift—or they may (in their effort to change) end up doing a 360° and wind up right back where they started. The problem is that when we create too much change too quickly, we end up lacking the foundation and framework for it to last. The 1° Shift is a seamless solution to the answers you seek.

When seeking out things that will make you happier, healthier, and more fulfilled, you must recognize that it's the tiny daily shifts that truly make the biggest impact. The thing is 1° shifts compound just like money in a compounding interest account. At first, it's easy to think nothing big is happening, but over time, the progress is huge. It will continue to support you and your long-term efforts.

Making these small 1° daily shifts might seem pretty insignificant at first. It might even be tempting to "skip" a few days, but know this: success depends on you *not* cutting corners. Cheating the method hurts no one but yourself. You must commit not just to the method but also to yourself, if you truly desire change. You *must* see the vision, and you *must* trust the process.

Visualize this: Your life is on a train track. This train track is your life's timeline. Your train track timeline began when you were born, and your past thoughts, actions, and experiences have moved you along this timeline you call your life. Have you ever wanted to change something, but no matter what you did, you just couldn't change or shake that old story or reality? This happens because you are stuck in your old timeline and your old ways of "doing." These ways no longer serve you. Deciding to apply the 1° Shift Method to your life is recognizing that there are other possible tracks available to you and your life. Making the first 1° Shift can instantly reroute you to a new destination. One moment that train is headed to New York City, and in the flip of a switch, it is now going to Florida. Because of this instant shift, you can begin operating from your new timeline immediately after you make your commitment to the shift. At first, it may seem like you are still going to your old destination because you're in the same train with the same passengers (house, body, friends, family, job, etc.), but over time, the scenery will begin to change, and you'll begin to see evidence that the shift is working. The change you made is truly bringing you to a new place. The 1° Shift Method is not just merely about the final destination. It is equally about the journey.

How do we know when to make this shift? What do we actually focus on to get where we want to go? And finally, how do we have a joyful experience in the process?

That, my friend, is what this book is all about.

We will look at where you are, where you want to be, and find the blocks that are keeping you from getting there. We will uncover the sneaky ways you miss tiny opportunities to make the shifts you need and begin to recognize how close you truly are to getting everything you've ever wanted. We will do this all without disrupting or uprooting your entire life in the process.

Many of us have a hard time seeing change, especially positive change in our lives. It's easier to focus on negativity and what isn't working than it is to recognize what actually is. The 1° Shift Method will help you to not only begin to see the positives in your life but to feel them, as well.

This is what sets the 1° Shift Method apart from everything else out there. When you begin to make tiny shifts, your perspective and feelings will also shift. You'll begin to notice more clarity in your thoughts, more courage in your daily tasks, and more general confidence than ever before. This is how the 1° Shift Method changes lives.

2

FROZEN IN TIME

"Time is really the only capital that any human being has, and the only thing he can't afford to lose."
~ Thomas Edison

*T*ake an outsider's look at your life as it is right now. Look at your job, relationships, financial status, health, hobbies, and anything else you may find in your life at this moment. When you observe all that is, what do you see? How do you feel?

If your life was frozen in time at this very moment, would you be happy? Do you want to live the rest of your life as it is right now? I am going to go out on a limb and say that your answer is no. If you're not happy with everything you have and all that you are, why haven't you changed it? The answer is simple: Change is scary, hard, and messy.

You may know that you're ready to make a shift in your life, but then, all of those "what if's" start to pop into your head. Fear soon takes root. What kind of life might be on the other side of something new and different?

See? Scary. The very idea of change can cripple people and make them go into a state of panic. Fear can make a person want to stand still and not make any forward progress. No matter how unhealthy or terrible the situation is, fear can make you desperately hold onto something familiar, even if it's less than favorable—and even if it's toxic.

No matter how volatile a situation is, most people won't make a change until an internal shift happens first. That innate knowing that we *must* do something, *anything* other than staying where we are. After all, why change something if we can tolerate it? People often learn to just accept things the way they are when they're not sure what else they can or should do.

One way to welcome a tiny shift or moment of awareness is to notice how you feel inside your body at any given time during the day.

Here's a quick exercise: Think of one thing you'd like to shift in your life. Sit with the idea of that specific thing for a good while and then become aware of how it makes you feel in your physical body. You may feel butterflies in your stomach. Your palms may sweat a bit, your heart may race, or your breathing may become shallow. Your mind may begin to chase the possibilities, or you may just abandon the exercise and stop prematurely.

Pay particular attention to whatever you're feeling. Do you think the driving force is fear or excitement? The funny thing is, fear and excitement present themselves physiologically in a very similar fashion. Yet, although they feel the same in the physical body, the *energies* of the two are very different. Excitement is expansive, open, and fluid, while fear is restrictive and preventative. It's important to really examine the energies you feel and where they come from. People often mistake excitement for fear and sometimes fear for excitement. Getting to know the cues of your body is one of the most important things you can do for yourself.

Once you've developed a form of physical awareness, you can quickly recognize whether what you're feeling is fear or excitement. When it's fear, your breathing gets shallow, your chest tightens, and your shoulders feel heavy. When it's excitement that you feel, your breathing gets deeper, your chest opens up, and your shoulders feel light.

Now, let's look at this from a practical standpoint. If you know that change is what you need and want, then staying where you are is exponentially worse than welcoming a shift. This is true for *any* area of your life. Think about it: How did you get to where you are now? Your past thoughts and actions brought you here to this moment. That's it. Staying where you are without applying any action in the direction of change means that you will be perpetually living the life your past has set up for you. You will be stuck on *this* track forever. Is that your goal?

The good news is that if you do indeed desire a shift, the power is yours. You don't have to stay stuck. You can kick yourself out of your old cycles and break up with the conflict (internal and external) that you've been living with. The 1° Shift Method offers a way to find the tiny moments of opportunity you need.

A VIEW ON CHANGE

Spend a few moments reflecting on your past association with change, both welcomed and uninvited. A few uninvited changes from my life were getting kicked out of the house, the death of my mother, and later on, the death of my father. Each of these uninvited changes turned my life upside down. Uninvited change is the story of life. Changes impact our lives in ways that we don't realize and can leave us feeling victimized. This was certainly true for me in all three of my examples. It's no wonder we resist change.

A welcomed change, however, is something different. We experience welcomed change when we quit that job we hated so much, stop spending time with someone who was toxic to us, or even when we finally go back to work after having a baby, that results in feeling a strange dichotomy of grief and relief. Welcomed change can take its own kind of toll. It can still be scary, hard, and even messy. Yet, it is through change that a person can realize new things about themselves and appreciate their resilience.

It's easy to get accustomed to the mundane routines that run our lives. This makes it challenging to step away from our routine and comfort zone. Habits that have served us in the past have a stronghold founded in the familiar. We innately trust what we know. Routines are known behavior. They are habits that have served us in the past. Whether they know it or not, most people seek routine and thrive with structure. There is safety in knowing what to expect. It conserves energy and allows us to believe we have control over our lives, even if just for a moment.

Welcomed change can be difficult to implement even when it must happen for our own greater good. I experienced this first-hand a few years ago after adopting my dog, Tank. I used to walk him three or four times a day, but when it got too hot in the summer, he didn't like to go outside. I knew the solution was to get up earlier in the morning and walk him. While this threw off my morning routine, it was a welcomed change for Tank and his wellness.

I gave up my late nights for Tank's greater good. This was what was needed, and I didn't like it, but eventually, I realized that this was a welcomed change for me, too. The change itself wasn't the hard part—it was the *act* of change that was difficult because it took me out of my comfort zone. I had to keep reminding myself that mindset and self-control are essential elements to producing change for the greater good.

Evaluating what *was* working and what *wasn't* working allowed me to create an internal shift in my mind and energy, which in turn, enabled an external shift of action. I knew what action needed to be taken for my continued success. From there, self-control and accountability became the work at hand. It's important to remember that change is an on-going battle. If you want to change your results, you must change the behaviors that are producing them. This is as true for small things like walking a dog as it is for big things like improving your health, building trust in relationships, and becoming financially independent.

A LESSON FROM NATURE

What is the most seamless way to make gradual, focused progress? Arguably, the best way to illustrate the thinking behind this concept is nature itself. Nature, like the universe, is in constant motion. Think of the monumental change that occurs over the four seasons. It's a slow, gradual process. It's all natural, fluid, and in sync. One tiny, beautiful shift each day —each hour

Implement change in your life in the same way. Change like the seasons. It won't happen all in one day—it happens incrementally, 1° at a time, one tiny beautiful shift at a time. During the year, it gradually gets warmer, and then it gradually gets colder. In the summer, it stays light out a little bit longer each day, and in the winter, it gets darker a little bit earlier each day. When that happens, does it feel overwhelming? Do you freak out because your life has become drastically different? No. For the most part, we don't even notice these daily changes (until we take them in collectively) because they are so small.

It is worth the effort to apply this understanding to the change in your life. Thinking of change this way makes these shifts tolerable. It makes them feel natural, easier to receive, and effortless to embrace. This view can help make change less complicated to implement and maintain. Lasting change is the result of making 1° shifts consistently over time. Don't expect to do it all at once. Do it gradually and do it in small increments. Take a little step each day, aligning first with your mind and then with your actions.

If you can stick with making incremental change for a duration of time, it will lead you to a completely different season. That is how you climb your Mount Everest; that is how you achieve the seemingly impossible. Focus on improving just one thing. Be willing to let go of your current season so that you can step into the season ahead of you!

3

PRIORITIES

"How we spend our days, is of course, how we spend our lives."
~ Annie Dillard

e're going to begin this chapter with an exercise.

1. Take out three pieces of paper.
2. On the first piece of paper, write out the top four things you spend the most time on during the day, outside of your main occupation. This could be driving to work, looking at social media, caring for kids/family, social engagements, etc. This is List 1.
3. On the second piece of paper, write out the four things you routinely do each day that are outside of true obligation. Such as, have your morning coffee, exercise, read, listen to podcasts, cook dinner, etc. These are things you generally do not negotiate out of your routine. This is List 2.
4. On the last piece of paper, write out your top four life priorities. These are things you feel you must have to achieve a "successful" life. Examples include financial

independence, healthy lifestyle, and being a good parent. This is List 3.

Now, place these three lists side by side.

Do any of the items on the lists match up?

It is a harsh reality when you realize what you spend your time on each day has little to do with your highest priorities.

Why is that?

It's all too easy to get up, throw yourself into the daily grind, work all day, come home exhausted, make dinner, clean the house, dive into your phone, go to bed, and wake up the next day to do it all over again. Unless we intentionally create goals and focus on our long-term ambitions, we tend to just focus on what's right in front of us. Doing this day-in and day-out becomes a habit—a habit that will keep you from crafting your life by design.

You must craft your day! You must design your life! But how?

Stephen R. Covey wrote a fabulous book called *First Things First*. It discusses the concept of The Four Quadrants and how our lives are molded by what we do each day, both consciously and subconsciously.

Covey helped me recognize that if I didn't put money first, I was always going to be in debt. If I didn't put my health first, I would always be too tired to do anything. If I didn't put my family first, I couldn't connect with my kids and partner, or support them.

Gaining clarity on these concepts helped me to create a life by design.

THE FOUR QUADRANTS

In the book, Covey explains how our priorities can be organized into four quadrants.

Quadrant #1: Important And Urgent

This includes legitimate crises, such as a heart attack, the transmission going out of your car, or damage from a water heater leak. This is anything that is coupled with urgency, high-stress, or deadline-driven.

Quadrant #2: Important But Not Urgent

This quadrant includes components that require preparation, such as saving money, eating right, meditation, exercise, creating a strong spiritual practice, and relationship building. These tasks take time but are not pressing.

Quadrant #3: Not Important And Urgent

This includes relations with other people: interruptions, calls, emails, or popular activities you feel you may be missing out on if you don't participate.

Quadrant #4: Not Important And Not Urgent

This is stuff that includes social media, phone calls, or binge-watching television. These activities can have value if they are uplifting or being done with other people, but by themselves, they tend to be time-wasters and fit into the fourth quadrant.

Take note that the lines aren't strictly drawn here. As an example, recently, I watched a movie with my son's girlfriend. This might seem like a quadrant four activity, but in reality, it was a quadrant two activity because it was a relationship builder as the time and activity were selected intentionally to be shared with one another.

HOW DO YOU SPEND YOUR TIME?

Most people spend their time in quadrants one and three. They deal with the urgent stuff first and spend their time putting out fires, whether they are important or not. Then, they numb themselves in quadrant four when tired and depleted. The truth is, we live in a world that is dominated almost entirely by activities in quadrants one and three. This is why it can be difficult to focus on what's really important. If a person can learn to live in quadrant two and prioritize their day, they can then begin to recognize their life's possibilities.

Here's an analogy for you: A professor stands at the front of the classroom with two empty containers. In the first container, he adds as many big rocks as he can fit and asks the class if it's full. The students say that it is. He then pours in some small pebbles. The students agree that now it is full. Then, he adds sand. Okay, now it's full. Then he adds water. Now the students realize that they were wrong each time until *finally*, the container is totally full. In a second container, he pours the sand in first. Then, he pours in the pebbles and water, but now the rocks can't fit. What does this all mean?

Picture it like this:

- The Sand—This is other people's problems (Quadrant #3).
- The Pebbles—This is the crisis stuff (Quadrant #1).
- The Water—This is mindless time-wasting (Quadrant #4).
- The Rocks—These are your main priorities (Quadrant #2).

Now, look at the professor's second example again. When everything else is dumped into the cylinder, the rocks will not fit, even though the rocks are the core priorities of your life—health, finances, peace of mind, well-being, and relationships.

If you don't put them in first, you're in real trouble. You will always be putting everyone else's stuff in front of yours, and your top priorities will never fit. Where will that leave you? You will live in the margins of your own life.

Now, go back and look at the first example. It's natural to assume that our priorities will take up all of our time, but that's not true with prioritization. You must become disciplined at putting your priorities at the front of the order. This is a *must* for crafting your day *and* your life.

THE LAW OF THE FARM

These realizations are extremely important, but they are only half the battle. Before you can change and plan, you need to have a clear understanding of some basic principles. It is easy to set your sights on List 3, but with strategy, we can ensure that our priorities are true priorities. If we want substance, we have to nurture it.

On a farm, you have to decide what to plant and cultivate. The same is true for your life. Top priorities are the seeds. After planting seeds, you have to tend to them, water them, and nurture them. Even if you can't see their initial growth, you don't just dig them up. You are a farmer, and you must have faith that they've sprouted roots and will thrive. When you tend to yourself on a daily basis, you too will start to establish roots and thrive. That is what Quadrant #2 and the big rocks are all about. They're about creating life by your design, in accordance with your dream. This is also what the 1° Shift Method is all about.

You are responsible for you and you alone. You are responsible for your happiness. Read that again: *You* are responsible for *your* happiness. You can't worry about having to make someone else happy, and you can't rely on someone else to make you happy. If something is making you angry or throwing you out of your happy place, it is your responsibility to address it.

Take a closer look at the word "responsibility." Covey breaks the word down into "response" and "ability." This basically means that you have the ability to make a response to anything in your life. To me, this translates to the idea that you have the ability to change *anything.* Whether you're eliminating bullshit, ending bad habits, or creating new ones, you have the ability to be responsible for your own life—and yes, you have the ability to change.

EXERCISE: THE BLUEPRINT FOR SIGNIFICANT CHANGE

Using the three lists you created at the beginning of this chapter, you can begin to craft a blueprint for the life you truly want to create.

The key is to take your top four life priorities (list 3) and marry them into the things that take up the most time during your day (list 1) and those things you MUST do each day (list 2). The goal is to be very intentional about not just *what* you're doing in a given day but also *why* and *how*. It is this type of focus that will allow you to create the daily life you most desire.

For example, if family connection is one item on your priority list, and you have "caring for my kids and making food / cleaning house," on list 1, you can choose to be more intentional with the time you spend with your kids and ensure that you're fully present with them while you're together. You can also invite them to help you with cooking and cleaning to nurture a strong bond and connection.

If you have education or self-help on your priority list, and you also have a 30-minute commute to work each day, you can add listening to self-help books while you travel to work.

When going through this exercise, you must be willing to think creatively about your lists and how you can incorporate strategic actions that will intentionally align you with your priorities. Keep in mind that this is an ongoing exercise, it is a way of being, as your priorities will change throughout your life. While I was raising my kids, my list looked entirely different than it does now that I'm an empty nester.

Before diving into creating your new set of lists, let me share with you my current top four priorities and some ways I am intentional about my time and activities:

1. Family / Friend Connection—Kids, Family, and Partner

- Snapchat my kids daily
- Write notes to my partner and family members
- Have lunch with my girlfriends / sisters
- Travel to visit my kids every few months
- Go on weekly adventures with my partner (hikes, antiquing, etc.)

2. Wealth Building—Through Investments and Education

- Review financial accounts daily
- Only buy on Amazon.com once a week
- Listen to podcasts and audiobooks about wealth, finance, and business-building
- Meet with my financial advisor quarterly

3. Health—Physical, Mental, Emotional, and Spiritual

- Work out or stretch daily

- Meditate
- Take high-quality supplements
- Get 7-8 hours of good sleep each night
- Eat mindfully
- Drink water
- Visit a therapist monthly

4. Being in a High Vibe state of Joy [Note: High Vibe does not mean high energy—High Vibe is feeling in flow with life]

- Pre-plan my workday
- Prep my morning routine the night before
- Keep my home clutter-free
- Do something daily that makes me laugh (listening to a comedian, or watching funny videos online)
- Listen to upbeat music daily
- Talk with my kids (we always have the BEST conversations)
- Talk with my "Peeps" (God and everyone in the ethers who help me out daily)
- Stop doing anything that makes me feel icky, heavy, or overwhelmed
- Avoid toxic situations and people

Most people forget to put themselves in the top four. That is why so many people are overweight, in challenging relationships, tired, and in debt. People forget that they have a choice and that they create their own reality. That's why people struggle to change because they don't think about what they *really* want, and they aren't intentional in focusing their actions accordingly. Instead, they are putting out fires all day long or just getting by.

I encourage you to take some real time (right now) to work through this exercise. The goal is to get a true understanding of what you want, and then visualize the way achieving this would make you feel. Take great care to consider the specifics of the life you most desire.

With that said, begin again:

- List 1: Write out the top four things you spend the most time doing.
- List 2: Write out four things you WILL or MUST do each day.
- List 3: Write out your top four priorities.

Be very intentional about what you put on these lists and use them to begin crafting a life you're excited about.

In the next chapter, we will look at those things that take up time and energy in our life that we just can't seem to prioritize or shake—you know, that stuff that is just plain bullshit—yeah, it's time to deal with that.

PART II
BULLSHIT

4

EVERYONE HAS PROBLEMS

"Advance confidently in the direction of your dreams."
~ Henry David Thoreau

Imagine what it might feel like if any of the following things were to happen to you today:

- Receiving a cancer diagnosis
- Getting fired from your job
- Your doctor telling you that you have pre-diabetes
- Your spouse telling you that he/she wants a divorce
- A loved one passes away

Ouch! These things are scary and can throw anyone into a tailspin.

Over the course of more than 20 years of coaching, I've learned that most people will not change until they hit a breaking point in their life. This usually means something disastrous has just happened, and they feel cornered and knocked off their feet. Unfortunately, once these things happen, only then do people decide to change, but at that point, it can sometimes be too late.

On the road leading up to the breaking point, it is easy to complain about the things that aren't going right without doing anything to take genuine action. Everyone has excuses. In the end, you either want it badly enough to take action, or you don't.

We all know what it's like to struggle. We've all been there: The car doesn't start. Your work is unappreciated. You don't get enough sleep. You overeat. You under-eat. You feel a lack of direction. Maybe your friends are not there for you, or you feel you can't live up to the expectations of others. Maybe you're the person who puts on a happy face even when things really aren't okay. Perhaps you're behind on your bills or are living with the fear of losing your job.

These things add up to the pressure you feel daily, and it is this pressure that makes looking to the future and pre-planning seem out of the question. The more you think about the things that are going wrong in your life, the more overwhelmed you feel. So, you dive into a streaming service or just pop on social media and begin scrolling. You avoid.

We all have dreams and aspirations for our futures. We all have things we want to achieve in life. Yet, before we can work on improving our future, we have to make sure we are dealing with the problems that exist in the present. You have to deal with all the BS in your life. You have to be able to recognize what exactly is keeping you from focusing.

Everyone has bullshit, and bullshit comes in many forms. We all have demons, but why do we put up with it for so long before addressing it?

Believe it or not, sometimes we don't even realize the amount of bullshit in our lives. We're so busy doing so many different things that we don't recognize what is helpful and what is hurtful. It isn't until we take a step back and analyze our lives that we can finally see what's actually going on. Sometimes, when this happens, we even say out loud: *"Wow, this is some serious bullshit—I can't believe I'm putting up with this!"*

Other times, we're aware of the bullshit, but we simply tell ourselves that it isn't *that* bad. "It's just a little bit of weight. It's not a big deal." We allow someone to overstep a boundary because we don't want to ruffle any feathers. We worry about what might happen if we start to address some of those issues and actually put our foot down. Addressing the bullshit in your life might cost you a friendship, an opportunity, or turn your life, temporarily, upside down.

Sometimes, it can be easier to "wait it out" when dealing with bullshit. We hope that our problems will go away on their own. That is especially true in relationships. It's easy to think, "I've invested so much time here that I don't want to give up now or throw in the towel." Or you might think you just need a new strategy, saying "Let me just try this one thing." It's easy to feel like you can change or save a person. Yes, you may love a version of that person, but if there's more bullshit than love and consideration, then you have a problem.

Dealing with a problem is not controlling a situation, and it's not spinning around in circles. Putting up with bullshit and just accepting things as being the way they are is not dealing with a problem. Conceding to the idea that a situation *is what it is* is not helpful. It's the first step to becoming uncomfortably comfortable. All the while, things get worse, and your life becomes harder and harder to change.

CALLING OUT YOUR OWN BULLSHIT

Tough love time. It's important to remember that a lot of the bullshit in our lives is self-inflicted. If you're unhealthy, in debt, or even in a toxic relationship, you must recognize that, on some level, you've put yourself there. This is a harsh reality that we all need to be willing to hear. So, why do we let these things creep up on us? How can we begin to truly pursue the life we've always wanted? How does one attain a healthy body, loving relationships, and a bank account balance that keeps financial stress at bay?

By taking action.

Tony Robbins came from nothing! Oprah came from nothing! They were tired of the bullshit in their lives and chose to take action. They were determined to go out and seek something better. They made a personal choice to improve their situation and go after what they wanted. And this isn't just true for spotlight celebrities, it's also true for millions of amazing individuals across the world and throughout history.

If you blame someone else for whatever is bringing you down, your situation will never change. Successful people don't look to blame others. They don't get stuck focusing on the problem. They recognize it, and then they put their energy into finding a solution that will bring them closer to achieving their goal. They recognize that opportunity lives in the situation, and they take action.

Henry David Thoreau once said, "Advance confidently in the direction of your dreams." When you decide to advance, the universe conspires to make it happen for you, but you have to stop blaming others and begin to believe in yourself. You must trust what your heart is telling you. You must be willing to do one thing different or better each day.

Be willing to pivot just 1° with awareness, and you'll begin to see real results. Take tiny intentional action and know that this entire process begins when you are prepared to get real, raw, and honest about the specific details that are holding you back from your happiness.

Once you begin identifying all the clutter in your life, it can be overwhelming. It can make you feel like you are even further away from the place you want to be—but you're not. You don't need to do everything at once. Change isn't going to happen overnight. It's a process that occurs with small, baby steps— tiny shifts in your behavior and perceptions. These shifts accrue over time, bringing you closer to the life you want.

I know what you're thinking. "That's great, Flora, but where do I begin?" Well, it all starts with being honest with yourself and calling out the bullshit. Ask yourself, "What is truly overwhelming me right now?"

Be willing to sit with the answer.

My divorce was finalized in 2013. My husband and I had been together for eight years, but it wasn't until the last year of our marriage that I realized I was in a very unhealthy relationship. Honestly, I didn't realize how unhealthy it was until quite a while afterward.

I was having lunch with a friend a few years after my divorce was finalized, and we started talking about our past relationships. She said, "You do realize that you're codependent, right?" I had no idea what she was talking about, so I had to Google it. When I had earned my life coach certifications, we briefly touched on codependency, but we didn't do an in-depth study on it. I was still in the dark, and I certainly had not identified that behavior in myself.

Well, that day, it clicked. I was forced to look at my relationships in an entirely different way. It was eye-opening to learn that I fit the description of a codependent person beautifully. For example, I used to hate how my ex would never answer any of my questions directly. I would ask him a question, and he would answer a question that I never asked. Whenever I challenged him, he would become angry, walk away, and give me the silent treatment for a week or two. He manipulated me in a way that destroyed my self-esteem and confidence. From this, I made excuses for him, and I convinced myself that it was still in my own best interest to stay with him.

I had to work really hard to get outside of that way of thinking and begin to see the things he was doing, as well as the motivation behind them. Finally, I realized staying in that relationship was exponentially worse than getting a divorce. I would rather feel terrified on my own than stay stuck in a relationship that put me down rather than build me up. I was manipulating him as much as he was manipulating me because I chose to conform to who he wanted me to be. This didn't help anyone build a desirable life. Codependent people often navigate their lives so that they can get what they *think* is best for them in the short term, not actually what *is* best for them in the long run.

After my divorce, I became excited at the prospect of having truly healthy relationships. I began actively working on my codependency through CODA.org and attending local meetings. I gained a better understanding of myself and my actions, and all my current relationships benefited as a result. My friends were shocked to hear of my codependency as in other areas of my life, I was completely independent!

Codependency comes in two forms: overt and covert. The overt involves one person openly controlling the other, whereas covert behavior involves the codependent individual acting as a chameleon, morphing into the type of person they think the other person wants them to be. The covert oftentimes does not confront others because they don't want to ruffle any feathers or upset others. It was hard for me to admit, but I was the chameleon. This covert behavior was my Achilles' heel. The biggest piece of bullshit in my life was in my intimate relationships, and change didn't occur until I was honest with myself about it.

This was such an important revelation for me to make because I wasn't being myself in all aspects of my life. I had to start being true to myself, and this involved focusing on my emotional health. I was doing myself and all my future relationships a disservice by living this outdated, lesser version of myself.

I tell all of this to encourage you to give yourself permission to be authentic—100% true to yourself. Grant yourself permission to own your likes, dislikes, wants, and needs. This starts by calling yourself out on your bullshit. You must ask yourself how exactly are you holding yourself back? How are you impeding your best self on a daily basis?

It isn't until you honestly identify those impediments that you can begin to eliminate them for good and become intentional about creating the life you want. It's time to create a life you love.

HOW THE BULLSHIT PILES UP

Whether we're aware of the bullshit or not, it causes stress. To relieve that stress, we do what comforts us. We do what we can to temporarily reduce pain and frustration. Maybe it's an extra glass of wine. Perhaps it's a bowl (or pint) of ice cream. Maybe after a fight with your partner, you turn to a friend or an attractive coworker who pays extra attention to you. Maybe you have mistrust in your relationship and find comfort in sneaking a look at your partner's phone. All of these acts are coping mechanisms that provide some temporary relief. They help us feel more in control of a situation that is actually out of control.

Coping mechanisms like these can quickly become habits, and in many cases, create more problems. Then, we have more bullshit that we have to deal with later on. What first started as a harmless pint of ice cream or a "meaningless" emotional affair can grow into a much bigger problem and get us into some real trouble. The kicker is that none of those coping mechanisms ever fix the original problem. They're just distractions we use to bury our heads in the sand—they're sidetracks that actually inhibit us from dealing with the real issue. Coping mechanisms like these can easily become a vicious cycle that worsens. Soon, all of that bullshit begins to strain the soul and become detrimental to our physical health. It creates stress fractures that damage our energy. Then, suddenly, one day, we look around and realize *this is a train wreck. How did this even happen? How did I get to this place?*

It can be overwhelming and seem impossible to fix, which creates a sense of hopelessness, but I promise you, there is hope! No matter what bullshit you are contending with, there is a way to get through it.

TYPES OF BULLSHIT

Bullshit can come in many different forms and at various times in our lives. Bullshit drains our energy, time, and attention. Our lives are full of it, but it can be difficult to identify *any* of it. It is often the things we are ignoring for the time being because we either haven't looked for a solution or have more pressing matters with which to deal.

We become so accustomed to our bullshit that it can be difficult to identify. Between work, family, friends, relationships, responsibilities, and home, we have a lot going on! Problems find their way into our lives, and when they go unaddressed, they linger and grow into something bigger. Just think about how quickly dirty dishes can pile up in the sink if you don't stay on top of them. That's the nature of the things that we ignore—they manifest into varying degrees of chaos in our lives.

Here, we will look at the five types of clutter that create bull-shit in our lives:

#1: Environmental Clutter

When we walk into a room, and it's filled with things that aren't put away, it feels disorganized and chaotic. University of California Los Angeles researchers Darby Saxbe and Rena Repetti's 2009 study "No Place Like Home: Home Tours Correlate with Daily Patterns of Mood and Cortisol" has proven that where there's visible physical clutter, there exists increased instances of indecision, stress, addiction, debt, obesity, and lack of sleep.

As a rule of thumb, we use only 20% of the things we own 80% of the time. Think about a time when you looked for something in your home, and after what seemed like way too long, you just gave up. You ended up buying a new version of the lost object, only to find it a few weeks later. It's frustrating. It wastes time and money and is one of the pieces of bullshit we can address. Environmental clutter causes us to become time-poor, distracting us from things that matter.

Thinking about the 80/20 rule, what items could you declutter from your personal environment today to help you feel more in control in your home? Theoretically, it means that you could get rid of a majority of your clothes, household items, and overall clutter, and you'd barely miss it. Think about that and ask yourself again: "What of the things in my immediate environment do I *really* need?" This is why the minimalist movement is taking the world by storm. I offer a decluttering program called "Simplify—10 Day Declutter Extravaganza!" to help you with this.

#2 Body Clutter

It's not just our homes and living spaces that can fall victim to clutter. Clutter plagues our internal world too, but you can get rid of it all the same way—you just need to know what you're looking for. It's easy to look at your living space and see all the physical clutter, so you know exactly what to tackle, but the clutter that lives inside your body is a little more difficult to spot. This requires that you tune-in and ask yourself, *how am I feeling today?*

To begin to recognize and become more self-aware of your body at any given moment, you can perform a simple body scan.

Begin by closing your eyes and taking a deep breath. Focus on your heart space (the place behind your breastbone). Tune in and become consciously aware of what you feel in that space. Take a few deep belly breaths. Allow your chest and belly to rise as you breathe in. Pause for a moment. Then, as you exhale, let your chest fall and your belly sink in. Continue to breathe deeply and scan your body. Start at the top of your head and work your way down to the bottom of your feet. Notice what grabs your attention. Notice if you're tired, have a headache, or are dehydrated. Pay attention if something hurts and how long it has been hurting. Do this without judging yourself. Observe what you notice. What new things are you suddenly aware of by paying close attention to your body?

Consider correlations that your mind makes for you. An ache in your foot might be indicative of your desire to move forward in your life, while a tense back might allude to a need for support. Pay attention to what body part grabs your attention and permit yourself to explore it. Notice the clutter that presents itself and be intentional about working with it to clear any unwanted energy. It is a great exercise of presence to check in with your body throughout the day to see how you actually feel and make tiny shifts accordingly.

Once you've practiced this exercise a few times, you'll become more and more self-aware of any disharmony that exists in your body. If you've only got a moment to give, you can breathe into your body with conscious awareness and ask, "What's one thing I can do to feel better at this moment?"

#3: Mental / Emotional Clutter

Mental and emotional clutter is closely linked to body clutter because the stuff we have going on in our brain triggers our emotional and physical selves. This type of clutter can come from past traumas, childhood experiences, and discomforts we haven't dealt with yet. The range is far and wide and can be as big as addiction or abuse, as ordinary as the need for a tough conversation, or as small as figuring out what to make for dinner. This type of clutter often manifests in the form of a never-ending to-do list and causes mental exhaustion and feelings of overwhelm.

When we carry a high number of "things" in our brains and also understand the weight of our choices, it can be easy to begin overthinking everything. Continually overthinking taxes the brain and impedes decision-making abilities, creating mental clutter in a hurry.

Many people suffer from what's called decision fatigue. Studies prove[1] that our decision-making declines throughout the day. In the morning, our brains are sharp, and as the day progresses, decisions become more difficult and require more energy. This leads to fatigue. When we're feeling overwhelmed, stressed, and preoccupied, that takes up brainpower.

We can deal with this clutter through journaling, hiring a life coach, or visiting with a mental health professional regularly. This will help you to build perspective on your life and keep your focus dialed in on what's important.

Clearing *all* kinds of clutter can sharpen decision-making abilities and help to maintain a state of flow, which inevitably helps to make progress on the path from where we are to where we desire to be.

#4: Digital Clutter & Digital Hoarding

Digital clutter and digital hoarding are tremendous issues in today's age. We are so much more reliant on technology and devices than we were even a few years ago. Consider how many devices you use throughout a typical day. How many notifications do you get in an hour? How many emails do you receive daily? Don't forget about the demand that Instagram, Twitter, or Facebook puts on your time too. This kind of clutter can be incredibly disruptful to your energy. It can take you out of your daily routine and even create the false idea that you have way too much going on. Much of this clutter is unnecessary.

It's a valuable practice to consider what digital actions cause your energy to drop. You can check in with your body and energy and ask, "Why does this feel (hard, heavy, overwhelming, etc.)?" Prepare yourself to be honest and open with what pops into your mind—this is your intuition helping you out. Once you've honed the ability to recognize what you need and why you need it, you can make a plan to release the clutter.

One simple way to regain perspective is to unplug from your devices. Try it for a day, a weekend, or even a week. One of my friends unplugged for 40 days during a religious holiday, and when she came back, she gained an entirely new relationship with the digital intrusions she allowed in her life.

When you're accustomed to clutter, you fail to see how chaotic, overwhelming, and negatively impacting it can be. Obviously, it's impractical to cut yourself off from technology altogether, but taking some focused time away can truly help provide the perspective you need to take ownership over your use of digital devices.

A client booked me for a month-long VIP experience to help her revamp her business. During our first meeting, we sat at her table brainstorming ideas in a document when her phone dinged. She picked it up, checked the notification, put it down, and started to work again. Over the next five minutes, she was interrupted by phone notifications 37 times (I counted). When I brought this to her attention, she admitted to being sick of all the interruptions. I agreed. We decided that it was within her power (and right) to mute her phone when she had a prioritized task to do. When she did just that, she got so much done that day and felt relief in her newfound freedom.

It's important to take time and recognize the things you're allowing in that don't belong. Digital hoarding is the act of keeping digital information in excess and beyond reason due to the belief of needing it again in the future. This can include emails, photos, apps, and old documents. The very idea of deleting or purging this content holds anxiety for a digital hoarder. Therapy is a wonderful way to overcome digital hoarding. Many people can do it on their own accord by following guidance or a plan.

Here are some convenient ways to declutter your digital life:

- Do an "Inbox Zero" once a week—go through and delete, answer, and process every single piece of email that comes into your inbox. If it's been too long, and you have 30,000 unread emails, hit "Delete All" and start fresh. (I promise, if it's important, they will email you back.) If that feels too scary, do an "inbox search" for the emails you know you may want to reference in the future and move those emails to their own folder. Then, delete the rest.

- Pare down your photos—print them, store them in the cloud, and remove them from your devices. If you are a parent of kids and animals, you can keep a favorites folder on your phone, but remove everything else.

- Review your apps, playlists, and digital books—keep only what you like and use. I get it, I love me some Audible, but dang, my collection was getting out of control. When I'm done reading a book, I now delete it from my device so that I don't have to scroll through all the titles I've previously read to find a new author. It helps me to know that my books are still safe in the cloud when I want to retrieve one. The same goes for music and apps—if you really miss it, you can always go back and get it.

- Curate an uplifting feed on your social media pages— unsubscribe, unfollow, unfriend, and remove yourself from any groups or associations that don't make you feel the way you want to feel. If you follow someone who creates posts that make you feel like shit or post things you really don't want to see, know that it is within your power (and your right) to disconnect.

These are great examples of small 1° Shifts. Trust me, taking ownership over digital clutter will make a difference in your life.

#5: Daily Clutter

Daily clutter is the chaos you experience throughout your day. The main reason this form of clutter piles up is because we haven't structured our day. Humans love routine because they find safety in them. When everything throughout the day is different, it's easy to burn through the glucose in our brains, which causes us to feel exhausted. Routines save mental and physical energy.

If we think back to our tribal roots, everyone in the community had a different job because each person was good at something different. That allowed people to conserve energy by not having to do the things they weren't good at. We don't live in a tribal environment anymore, but that primal part of our brain still exists and influences how we operate daily. When we don't have structure and focus, days can quickly become chaotic. It is chaos that depletes our energy stores.

When we look at daily clutter, we should look to be productive, not just busy. While busy work merely keeps us busy, productivity helps us achieve goals. It's easy to feel like you don't have time to do something outside of the norm (write a book, learn a language, lose weight, etc.) because you are "too busy." The key is to recognize which things are keeping you "busy" and to eliminate or streamline those things so that your time is better put to use.

A great way to manage daily clutter is to structure the beginning and the end of each day. When you approach your morning with focus and know exactly how you want to start your day, the rest of the day naturally becomes smoother. The same thing happens in the evening.

One way to put this into practice is to simply set an alarm one hour before you intend to go to bed and use this as a signal to begin prepping for the next day. These are things that don't take a lot of brainpower, yet still set you up for a smooth morning experience.

Routine and structure can create peace, calm, ease, and flow, and conserve vital energy in your brain. With structured routines at the beginning and end of each day, you're more equipped to handle unexpected moments of chaos when they arrive.

Here's a sample PM Routine: 1 hour before bed

- Tidy up kitchen: Do dishes, wash counters, dump the trash, fill up water bowls for pets
- Set out breakfast dishes and prep coffee/tea/protein drinks
- Check the weather for the next day and lay out clothes, shoes, and accessories
- If you have kids, have them pick out their clothes and decide on what's for breakfast
- Prepare for bed (shower/bath, brush teeth, change into pajamas)
- Get in bed and set your intentions for the next day

Sample AM Routine:

- Get up 15—30 minutes earlier than you normally would
- Reaffirm your intentions for the day and visualize it going smoothly
- Do one thing that lights you up
- Snuggle with your partner
- Have an orgasm
- Listen to a fun song
- Do some yoga
- Write in your journal
- Pray or meditate
- Listen to a motivational podcast
- Start your day

Looking at each category of clutter and allowing yourself to make mental notes on areas where the most bullshit in your life resides can be a refreshing experience. None of these changes require a commitment to yourself. They are just minor tweaks to your routine, some of which might only take minutes, even seconds of your day, but such changes can truly have a significant impact. Look for ways that you can slightly "shift" your routine, and notice how, over time, those "shifts" create lasting and recognizable change.

5

CREATING BOUNDARIES

"If someone throws a fit because you set boundaries, it's just more evidence a boundary is needed."
~ Unknown

*B*oundaries are created to ensure personal safety, comfort, and self-respect in different aspects of our lives. If boundaries are crossed by either ourselves or others, we may feel discomfort, anxiety, and anger.

Let's think of boundaries in a generic sense. Take road rules, for example. When cars were invented, it created unforeseen hazards and problems in traffic flow resulting in accidents. As it worsened, new rules and boundaries were set in place to protect drivers and pedestrians on the roadways. Now we abide by the rules. We drive on the specified right or left side of the road, depending on what country we are in. We stop at stop signs, we don't pass on a double yellow line, and we don't cross into oncoming traffic. All of these boundaries were established and are kept because of previous issues in driving history. Road rules were put in place to ensure that we can all drive safely while commuting to work, going on trips, or running errands.

Establishing personal boundaries is not so clear. What may seem like a healthy boundary for one person is not necessarily a healthy boundary for someone else.

We often cross another person's boundaries unknowingly. It's easy to assume when you're talking to someone that they have similar boundaries to the boundaries you hold (based on your own experiences and upbringing), but this is often untrue. External personal boundaries involve physical proximity and correlated emotional comfort level. Internal boundaries are where the gray area often resides. These boundaries include personal beliefs or the emotional capacity to handle sensitive subjects. All of these boundaries can be communicated through body language, and most often, are not spoken of at all. Boundaries exist in many different realms, including physical, sexual, emotional, mental, and relational areas. Generally speaking, boundaries are not simply a black and white matter, and they can easily be circumstantial.

Boundaries in relationships are typically the most important to set in place, but most of us enter into relationships without clearly sharing our boundaries. Some of the more common examples of crossing a boundary in a relationship is sharing too much (or everything) too soon, or the opposite, which is staying so closed-off that the other person has to dig around to learn anything at all. Interestingly, both of these scenarios are often born out of fear. People fear becoming so involved in another person's life that they might not be able to live without them. So, they either loosen their boundaries too far or set them too rigid. We give in to fear of rejection instead of talking about our feelings and establishing healthy relationships. When personal boundaries are permeable or unclear, it is called "enmeshment" and can only lead to destructive, unhealthy relationships.

The main reason why boundaries get crossed is because they exist in the first place. Without understanding where the line is set, it is easy to step into the "enmeshment" zone and hurt those around us. The second reason we cross the line is to test the limits of where the boundary actually is. Picture yourself walking into a museum exhibit and being told not to cross the rope. To your left, you see someone jumping over the rope, just to see what happens! They're testing the boundary to see what the outcome would be.

Boundaries are sometimes crossed with complete disregard. It's a person making a choice for selfish desires. The person is crossing the rope with destructive intent in place of curiosity.

The good news? There are ways to create a set of healthy boundaries for yourself.

Here are some quick steps to get you started:

1. Think about what feels good and bad in your life. Take note by writing these down. Recall past situations or relationships that have made you feel disempowered, like you didn't have a voice in the matter.

2. Based on the experiences you've written down for #1, create a set of rules, or boundaries, about your relationships (intimate and platonic) that feel empowering. For example:

- I don't hang out with drug users.
- I don't drink and drive.
- I only have monogamous intimate relationships.
- Don't enter into relationships that feel toxic or draining.

3. Create parameters like this for every aspect of your life where you feel you've given away your power or where you want to feel more self-assured in your boundaries.

Doing this exercise will allow you to establish where your healthy boundaries are and where they are not. It will also help you to better communicate within your current and future relationships.

WHEN BOUNDARIES ARE CROSSED

When our boundaries are crossed, we have two options: we can react, or we can respond. When we react, it often leads to defensive behavior that leaves us, or someone else, feeling hurt. Responding after someone crosses a boundary allows us to share our needs in a way that isn't triggering or accusatory. Responding helps establish a healthy boundary moving forward for yourself, and for the other person involved.

Like I've said in previous chapters, life is hard, and we all mess up (especially in the "enmeshment" zone) but learning your boundaries and establishing them clearly creates healthier communication for you and those around you. You might feel weary or scared about how someone will respond, or even worse, react, but you must be brave. It's helpful to think about what life would look like if people respected your boundaries. What would it feel like? How would your life be different? You owe it to yourself to create the life you want to live.

You can only be responsible for your boundaries. This is especially tough for parents. At the time this book is being written, my kids are 24 and 21, and I want them to be happy! I love to guard and guide them, but I'm not responsible for their happiness—they are. It's up to them to find what fulfills their lives. I can't sit in the blurred lines of the "enmeshment" zone and control from afar. I have to take responsibility and set clear boundaries for myself and respect the ones my kids have set too.

It can be particularly difficult to discuss boundaries with those who are closest to you, such as a spouse or a close friend. It can be hard to find the balance between speaking your truth and respecting the person in front of you, especially if you've been putting it off, and we've all been guilty of doing that at some point. Speaking your truth simply means being honest with yourself and the other person about how you feel without blame or implication.

When the time comes, and you've gathered your courage to have the tough conversation about boundaries, it can be helpful to prepare by using this dialogue script:

> "When_____ happens, I feel_____ because_____, and what I really need is _____."

When I first learned this, it was called an "anger script," but it can be used in more situations than just when you're angry. That's why I call it a "dialogue script." It's a helpful tool to find common ground with nearly every form of conflict. I found this script particularly helpful when speaking to my ex-husband. I have seen it work wonders with my client base, as well.

One client was having particular trouble communicating honestly with her husband when issues came up. One afternoon, she picked up their tax return that was sitting on the table and asked her husband a question about it. Instead of engaging in conversation, he reacted by grabbing the tax return, yelling at her, and storming out of the house. They didn't speak openly for two weeks. Her sense of defeat and confusion could be thoroughly felt when she said, "I don't even know what I did wrong."

After some discussion, I equipped her with the dialogue script and encouraged her to approach her husband. On a piece of paper, she wrote, *When I asked about the tax return, I felt hurt because I wanted some clarification and was confused about why you were yelling, but what I really need is for us to sit down and have a discussion about the taxes so that we're both on the same page.*

The crucial part of this dialogue script is taking the accusation of "you, you, you" out of the conversation and replacing it with ownership: "me, me, me." The idea is to bring the problem to the forefront but expressing how it makes you feel and why you feel that way while offering a possible solution. It can be easy to start using phrases, such as "you always do this," or "you never do this," and blame the other person. It only creates defensive walls and often escalates the situation. The real key to using the "dialogue script" is to offer a solution —not to create a negative spiral or another argument. The solution may not be finite or absolute, but at least the door will be open for possibilities and not missed opportunities due to using the "you, you, you" approach.

I shared this technique with another of my coaching clients, who was having a difficult time with an alcoholic spouse. They fought nearly every day. On a notecard, she scribbled down her dialogue script and practiced it over and over again. She never went anywhere without the notecard in her pocket or her bag—it was always close at hand. When she gathered her courage and recited the dialogue script to her husband during an argument, it stopped him in his tracks. Her response opened the door to common ground. Several weeks later, they got in another argument, and her husband was the one to stop and ask: "Wait, where's that notecard you had?"

"It's downstairs," she told him.

He broke the pattern by going downstairs to get the notecard and filling in the blanks for the dialogue script for how he was feeling. The next week she told me, "It works! Now we are talking and actually coming up with solutions. We figure stuff out, together."

The dialogue script breaks the negative cycles that we create for ourselves and helps us to communicate how we feel. When you're presented with a tough situation, write out the dialogue script, and fill in the blanks. How does it feel to say it out loud? How would you respond if these words were spoken to you? When you take a step back and break the pattern, it's much easier to see the solution you seek. It's also much easier to stop problems before they start.

How do we begin to address an issue if it isn't that big of a problem yet? Wouldn't it be "stirring the pot?" The answer is no. Most of us tend to not address the issue or decide to make a big change until we hit absolute rock bottom. When the final straw comes, we can't think clearly and end up lashing out and placing blame. It's easy to point fingers when this happens, but when we address the problem before it escalates, we can approach it calmly and work toward a possible solution, rather than reacting in anger.

Recognizing your own boundaries makes it easier to communicate how you are feeling. Without boundaries, you can fall into playing the victim. As a response, you create new coping mechanisms that don't always healthily address the issue. Soon enough, your coping mechanisms have turned into habits that cultivate a negative spiral for you and your relationships. The practice of creating boundaries is similar to that of forming habits—you have to rewire your brain by creating new neural pathways.

The dialogue script is a perfect example of how you can communicate boundaries (external and internal), while stripping away old habits and bullshit situations that you've previously labeled as normal to begin forming the future you want.

6

LEARNING TO SAY "NO"

"I don't say no because I'm busy. I say no because I don't want to be busy."
~ Courtney Carver

$\mathcal{P}$art of responding is the ability to say "no". Of course, we have obligations in life. There are tasks we have to do like care for children, pets, plants, etc. That is not what I'm directly referring to. I'm talking about the people who drag you under when asking for too many favors—the ones who block you from focusing on your own life or talk you into doing things you don't really want to do. I'm talking about all those situations where you say "yes" merely out of some form of pressure or ill-conceived obligation.

Much of what feels uncertain are the things that feel out of control for us. When we lack direction or move our boundary line, we limit ourselves from speaking our truth. Cheryl Richardson, one of my early coaching mentors, talks about how the lack of ability to say "no" does a huge disservice not just to ourselves but also to everyone else. Learning to say "no" strategically does not mean we should never say "yes". Cheryl compares this strategy to the safety instructions that flight attendants recite before a plane takes off. You've probably heard the following instructions countless times: "If you are traveling with a child or someone who requires assistance, secure your mask first, and then assist the other person".

Learning to say "no" isn't just a form of self-care—it's a way for you to truly and fully be capable of helping those around you. You must do a self-check first, what do you *need* in this situation? Just like on a plane, you can't control if the masks will deploy—or when. You will never be in control of every situation, but you can control what you choose to do in response to given situations, and you can honor your own needs in the process.

WE ARE "YES" PEOPLE

If you're reading this book, you are most likely a "yes person" or someone who always helps others first because that's your default reaction—even to your detriment. I know how you feel because I used to be this way too. I always said "yes" because I was afraid of being perceived as rude when saying "no". I wanted to please everyone around me and avoid conflict at any cost. I feared losing future opportunities as a result of saying "no". There were times I didn't realize why I was saying "yes" or even what I was saying "yes" to because it had become such a regular habit.

My older sister had this same problem. I got the chance to talk to her about it while we baked cinnamon rolls for my niece's ballet trip. When my sister asked for my assistance, I said, "Hell yes!" I love baking and knew I would enjoy learning the recipe for my sister's amazing cinnamon rolls.

While baking, we were talking about what was going on in her life. Her practice of saying "no" had recently been put to the test. My sister sings in the church choir and is the "go-to" person for weddings and funerals. She is also always the first person called to fill in when someone cancels or is sick. She was sharing with me that it had gotten to the point where she was doing at least one wedding or funeral every single week. "It's exhausting," she expressed, "but I'm learning to say 'no'."

"Yay! How's that been going?" I asked.

"It's weird because I don't want to piss people off, and I don't want anyone to think badly of me, but I think I'm getting the hang of it." She shared that she was getting resentful because they weren't asking her in advance. They would ask her the day before an event and just assume she'd be available. She even told the coordinator that she wouldn't be able to sing in July at all because I was getting ready for a trip with her daughter. "But the woman still kept asking even after I repeatedly told her that I couldn't."

I wondered for a moment, and then asked, "Well, how long had you been saying 'yes' to her before this?"

"About eight years."

Well, there you have it. That's why. My sister had become the default option, and people weren't used to taking "no" for an answer. She had conditioned them by always saying "yes".

"I really like being able to say 'no'," she said. "If I want to do something, I'll say 'yes', but now it's my decision."

You get used to saying "yes", and after a while, people come to expect that of you. It's a boundary we let people cross, again and again, and this allowance takes away from our own lives. When people repeatedly ask you after you've said "no", what is your response? Do you budge and side with their perspective after their inquisitive "why" comes up? Over time, this creates resentment in you, and eventually, this resentment creates more conflict, stress, and bullshit in your life. It's hard to break the habit, but responding truthfully and holding your ground keeps your power where it belongs.

HOW TO CREATIVELY SAY "NO"

People will approach you in every possible way when they want something from you. Favors and requests come over the phone, through email and text, and in person. Sometimes, people want an answer immediately; other times, you can get back to them at a later time. How you respond depends entirely on the situation.

Below are some creative ways to say "no":

1. "Well, I can't really commit to this right now because I have another priority."

This is what my sister did. She told her coordinator that she would be unavailable for the entire month of July because of a prior commitment. Remember, you don't have to explain yourself. Also, feel free to reword this response to fit your situation.

2. "Actually, now is not a good time. Maybe we can connect tomorrow, so I can look at my calendar."

This response is good to use when someone puts you on the spot in person, like approaching you in a grocery store. This buys you some time so that you can sit with the idea and figure out if it's something that you genuinely want to do. You can always call or email the person later if you have trouble saying no in person. Sometimes, the person might apply pressure by asking for a response immediately. This gives you a way to say "no" so that you don't commit to anything without fore-thought.

3. "Oh my gosh, this sounds really cool, but it's just not my thing."

This requires a little more honesty right up front. I'll give you an example. A friend of mine always asks me to go to networking events at 7 o'clock in the morning. Even though I love getting up early to start my day, I enjoy a slower start to my workday. To me, networking is working, and I'm just not ready to start my workday that early—and that is exactly what I say, *"Even though this sounds like a great event, I'm just not into going to things that early in the morning."* Just be honest, it's that simple.

This response is also good to give those who reach out asking you to participate in MLMs (multi-level marketing companies). I'm always sure to make my reasoning clear, *"I'm glad you're thriving, and this is working out for you, but this product really isn't for me. However, I'll keep you in mind if I think of anyone who might be a better fit."*

Referring to others is another way to say "no" when asked to volunteer for something that might not be your thing. "I'm not so sure that I'm the best person for the job, have you considered asking _____?"

THE MORE YOU DO IT, THE EASIER IT GETS

We've all been in situations where someone excitedly tells you about some event they need you for, but you already know your answer is a hard "no". It can be easy to slip back into saying "yes" in a face-to-face situation. It will take time and practice to say "no" and feel comfortable with it. If you're not ready for it in person, use one of the provided responses, and then follow up with a sincere reply over text or email. This practice gives you time to think and cultivate a response that says "no" with the best intentions.

It can be challenging to break any habit, but over time, the more practice you give to it, the more confident you will feel when you need it most. Draw upon the techniques discussed previously. If you dwell too long on the fact that saying "no" is uncomfortable and difficult, it will inherently be so every time you are presented with it. Instead, tell yourself, "*Saying 'no' has been challenging for me in the past, but it's getting easier. I've been learning to love myself enough and respect how I feel. It's important that I recognize when something doesn't resonate. In those situations, I will choose to do what is best for me. When I need to say 'no', I will do so with confidence.*"

Sometimes, it can be difficult to determine when you should say "yes" or "no". It's a good practice to listen to how you feel when someone asks you to do something. Does your energy drop? Do you feel excited? Pay attention to your initial reaction. When the answer isn't "hell yes," it should probably be "no." When you commit with a "hell yes," then you've found a situation that will lift you up, rather than one that drags you down.

Remember, when you say "no", the person doing the asking is in the exact same position as they were before they asked. Nothing has changed for them.

Re-read that last sentence again.

When you say "no", the person doing the asking is in the exact same position as they were before they asked. Nothing has changed for them.

The first time I heard this, it changed everything. It resonated deeply. Sure, the other person might be disappointed, but if someone gets upset because you said "no" to something you don't want to do, that is absolutely not your fault.

"No" is still a complete sentence, and more often than not, that is all you need to say. Own your "no."

7

SUCCESS IN SIMPLIFICATION

"Our life is frittered away by detail... simplify, simplify."
~ Henry David Thoreau

*W*hen will you begin to live the life you want? You've written lists about clearing your plate of clutter and written down healthy boundaries you want to keep. You've learned ways to say "no", and even still, it's all a lot of work. Let's keep it simple. Simplification is the key to taking control of your space, time, and energy.

Here's an exercise I do whenever my life feels chaotic and I'm not sure why.

Step #1. Do a brain dump.

A brain dump is taking all those thoughts in your head—the good and the bad—and releasing them. Everything that is stressing you out, pissing you off, or making you feel over-whelmed—write it all down.

What's on your to-do list? What are you avoiding? What's something you need to get out of your head? Oftentimes when

I do this, I have four or five handwritten pages filled with all the clutter that's been crowding my mind. Now, it's all laid out in rows on paper instead of jumbled in my mind.

Step #2. Find your number one stressor.

Take your brain dump and underline your top 10 stressors. Next, circle your top three, and then place a star by the number one thing that is stressing you out.

Most people get overwhelmed at this part. It can be scary walking through the whole process. Give yourself permission to feel what you need to as you work through this process.

Step #3. Look at that top stressor on your list and ask yourself the following:

1. How can I look at this stressor differently?
2. What's a possible solution to this stressor?
3. Am I willing to address this today?
4. What's one thing that I can do right now to begin to clear this?

Remember, the goal is to take control of your space, time, and energy.

SMALL PROBLEMS MATTER TOO

One day, not long after my kids and I had moved from Oklahoma to Wisconsin, I was feeling particularly stressed. I tried to pinpoint the cause but couldn't place my finger on it. I did the brain dump exercise. Six pages later, I looked at the items on my list, line by line. Eventually, I narrowed down my list to the single most significant stressor. I was shocked to find that the one thing that was stressing me out the most was cat litter all over the floor. Seriously! I know it sounds stupid, possibly superficial or petty, but I had put off addressing the problem for so long that it had built up itself up beyond measure.

When I lived in Oklahoma, the litter box was in the garage and never a problem to worry over. When we moved to Wisconsin, the litter box's new location was on the lower level. My bedroom was downstairs, so naturally, as soon as I'd get to the bottom of the stairs, there it would be: cat litter. No matter how much I swept, I was always stepping on cat litter. It was on the floor all the time, a constant and continual frustration. Seriously, it looked like the cats were celebrating Mardi Gras down there. Instead of throwing beads, they were throwing litter. When I realized this was my top stressor, I worked through the process of rectifying it.

#1: How can I look at this stressor differently?

This feels hard, and I can't. I do not want to look at this differently. Sometimes when I look at problems differently, solutions appear, and I can see a different approach. This time I don't see one popping up immediately.

#2: What's a possible solution to this problem?

I have to think. Hmm, what can I do so the cat litter isn't on the floor? I'm not going to get rid of the cats. I'm not going to train them to use the toilet. I figure the easiest solution for me is to get a rug to put under the litter box to catch the cat litter. Bingo!

#3: Am I willing to address this today?

Abso-freakin-lutely!

#4: What's one thing I can do right now to clear this stressor?

Get the rug today!

Once I had clarity of thought and a plan of action, I got to work. I measured the area to determine the square footage, found a local store that had rugs this size (thanks to a quick internet search), and purchased the rug. I came home, cleaned the floor, and put it down under the litter box. And bang! It worked. The problem was solved!

It doesn't matter how small or petty the problem might seem (yes, it is just cat litter), but if it's at the top of your stressor list, it is definitely a problem that's worth addressing. Sometimes, these little things can accumulate more frustration in your life than the big things. I promise you it's not worth putting off. You can do it. Clean up the mess. Fix the cabinet door that has been bothering you. Visit the person you need to see. Make the phone call you're avoiding. Whatever it is, work through the process. That's the quickest way to rescue yourself from bullshit situations and find solutions. When you've done the first item on your list, tackle the second item! Keep working through your list until your mind feels clear.

WHEN YOUR PROBLEM IS MUCH BIGGER THAN CAT LITTER

Unfortunately, not everything in life is as simple as solving a cat litter problem. There was another time I did a brain dump and had a much more severe problem at the top of the list—my codependency. Yes, that again. Identifying the issue was the first step. Now, I had to address it. I had to ask myself how much of a role it played in my life. I looked back at previous lists (a great reason to repeat this practice in the same notebook over time), and I came to realize that relationship issues with my significant other was a top stressor on nearly every list. I worked through the steps again:

#1. How can I look at this differently?

I have gone through therapy during all three of my marriages, and what I've learned is that mutual codependency led my partner and I to take each response personally, resulting in conflict and prompting withdrawal. This time around, I want to view my situation through the cause and effects of codependency.

#2. What is the possible solution to this problem?

I could attend a codependency anonymous meeting and work through the recommended 12-step process.

#3. Am I willing to address this today?

Oh, hell yeah! Sign me up.

#4. What's one thing that I could do right now to clear this stressor?

I could reach out to someone and have a conversation about codependency. I could start reading the CoDA literature and look at a calendar of available meetings and commit to one.

That is what I did. I decided I was done living in my own cycle of codependency and wanted to change. Since then, I've been through the 12-step process several times over. I've had sponsors and have been a sponsor and I still choose to go to meetings to keep issues at bay. The truth is, when our problems are bigger than cat litter, sometimes the solution is an ongoing affair.

We all engage in "sacred relationships." These sacred relationships are partnerships with people who bring out the best and the worst in us. We are paired with others to heal areas of our lives that can only be done alongside another person. A few examples of these sacred relationships are a cheating ex, a toxic stepparent, a soul sister, or a faithful partner. Each one of these people might bring out a different aspect of your soul or challenge your development in different ways.

If a relationship is toxic now, it doesn't mean it won't be healthy in the future, and because a relationship is healthy now, that does not mean it will always stay that way. All of our relationships are windows into our souls. Every relationship opens up opportunities for us to heal and become closer to our higher power. Walking away from addressing what we need will only hinder us and lead to grief and future heartache. When you deal with the stressors and problems you need to address, you allow yourself to lean into the work that needs to be done.

TAKE ACTION!

Lasting changes requires courage in action. Every time I feel myself getting stressed or overwhelmed, I grab my notebook. I commit to the process all the way through. I take action in how I want to live my life. The goal is to deal with one stressor at a time and repeat the process through each item on the list. This is how you use momentum in your favor. And remember, you are not meant to go through this life alone. If the thought of doing this feels overwhelming, reach out. Ask for support from a life coach, mentor, therapist, or someone else who has dealt with what you're going through. We have a fabulous group of women in my 1° Shift Tribe who help each other in eliminating the bullshit in our lives.

Support is the foundation of action. We can learn about what must be done all day long, but until it's put into action, you'll not see results. Reading another book, listening to another podcast, watching another video. None of these will make a difference in your life until you take what you are learning and put it to action!

PART III
HABITS

I am your constant companion.

I am your greatest helper or your heaviest burden.

I will push you onward or drag you down to failure.

I am completely at your command.

Half the things you do, you might just as well turn over to me, and I will be able to do them quickly and correctly.

I am easily managed, you must merely be firm with me. Show me exactly how you want something done, and after a few lessons, I will do it automatically.

I am the servant of all great men and alas, of all failures as well.

Those who are great, I have made great. Those who are failures, I have made failures.

I am not a machine, though I work with the precision of a machine plus the intelligence of a man.

You can run me for profit or run me for ruin, it makes no difference to me.

Take me, train me, be firm with me and I will put the world at your feet.

Be easy with me, and I will destroy you.

Who am I?

I am a habit.

~ Anonymous

8

YOUR HABITS

"What we do everyday matters more than what we do once in a while."
~ Gretchen Rubin

*L*et's take a moment to understand why we do the things we do and why it is so hard to change! Most people move through life stumbling over themselves in attempts to create lasting change. However, the more you understand how the brain works and how habits are formed, the more you can tune your brain to the life *you* want to live.

Everything we do in life stems from a need, impulse, or desire. We brush our teeth daily. We run errands around town. We make meals for ourselves and our family. We drink a glass of wine in the evening. We sing in the shower. We visit with friends. No matter what it is that you cultivate in your life, there are patterns that you repeat over and over. Habits are formed in thought and established through behavior. Some are intentional, some are situational, and some are a combination of both.

Imagine walking into a local cafe alone, and you notice there is one open seat in the back corner. The next time you go into the same cafe, you automatically head for that same spot, even if other seats are available. Each time you visit the cafe, you continue to sit in that spot. Eventually, people start to take notice, and someone walks up to you to ask why you always sit in the same spot. Naturally, you respond by saying why you choose to sit there: you focus well in that spot, it's close to the bathroom, you have associated it with good memories, etc. It feels familiar to you. You've created a safe space in the cafe and designated it as your own.

When growing up, we often develop habits by mimicking others. We seek approval from our parents or teachers by copying certain tasks, such as washing our hands or taking our shoes off after playing outside. Those habits are formed through observation and positive affirmation. Eventually, we do these things without thinking twice. The same goes for social habits. Some people order a beer when they are out with friends but rarely drink at home. Others only smoke when at a party and avoid it otherwise. We form social habits around the people we hang out with, and over time, nobody in the group ever questions how those behaviors began in the first place.

Work habits can also be like this. You may ritually get up to make a cup of coffee in the break room sharply at 11:00 a.m. Perhaps when you exit a meeting, the first thing you do when you return to your desk is to check emails and messages before getting back to work. These habits have become part of your process. Eating habits work the same way. Do you load your plate up now because food was scarce in your childhood? Maybe you help yourself to snacks before bed because you get hungry at night, or maybe you buy fast food because your schedule feels hectic.

Social media habits are among the most powerful of today's habits. Chances are you mindlessly check your news feed in the morning before getting out of bed, or you unconsciously begin your lunch break with a social media scroll.

What do you typically do before bed? Do you play games on your phone, read a book, watch TV, or have sex? These are all habits that form a pattern in your daily life. Everything we do every day becomes part of the life we choose to live.

How many of your habits hinder you from living the life that you want? Do you beat yourself up at the end of the day for not accomplishing your to-do list? Do you overeat (or under-eat) when you're stressed out? The way you talk to yourself about your habits has a significant impact on your life. This means habits have the power to not just affect you positively but also negatively. Just as habits can lift you, they can spiral down and get out of control.

Most of the time, we are not even aware of our habits. I once spoke with a woman who made a ham every year during a family function. She would cut off the ends, cover it in a sweet glaze, and pop it in the oven. Her husband particularly loved this tradition, but one day asked, "Why do you cut the ends off?"

She had to pause for a moment to consider why she did this. She replied, "I don't know. It's the way my dad taught me." To discover the mystery as to why it was important to cut the ends off, she called her father. "That's just how my mother used to do it," he told them. So, they called her grandmother to reveal the secret, and her response was, "I did it so it would fit in the pan!"

There were three generations of family members cutting the ends off the ham, and two of them had no clue why they were even doing it. While the grandmother did it out of necessity, the son and granddaughter followed suit out of habit. Our routines can easily follow this scenario. We do things without even questioning why we do them, and rarely stop to consider if the habit should continue.

In *The Power of Habit,* Charles Duhigg explains how people who have sustained certain types of brain injuries and memory loss could still perform habitual behavior, like routine tasks in their daily life, from washing their hands before eating or making coffee when they first wake up. Patients could not explain how to navigate to the kitchen, but when they were thirsty, they would walk into the kitchen and pour themselves a glass of water. It was a habit that their body remembered even when their brain couldn't explain why.

CAN HABITS HURT YOU?

Grab the notebook you had before and write down every regular habit you have. Write down every little thing you habitually do from the time you wake up to the moment that you fall asleep.

Once you've written it all down, look through your list and ask yourself how you feel about each item as a habit. Is it a good habit? A bad habit? A neutral one? In other words, does this habit hinder you or help you move forward into the life you want?

While reviewing your list, don't judge yourself. Use this as a time to become more aware of how you truly spend your day. Stephen R. Covey once posed this question: "What's the one thing you can do, if done every single day, that will make the biggest impact on your life?"

THE CRAFT OF HABIT

By watching amputees, plastic surgeon Dr. Maxwell Maltz determined it took them 21 days to adjust to not having their limb. You might have seen ads for a "21-Day Challenge" or programs titled "21 Days to a New You!" Many people have attempted the 21-day fad and were only left with disappointment. It's important to remember that 21 days is the minimum amount of time it takes to start a new habit.

In 2009, the European Journal of Social Psychology published an article about a group of people who had to choose between an activity or behavior that they had to repeat at the same time every day. The average time it took to develop a new habit for this group ranged between 18 to 254 days. There is a vast difference between 18 and 254 days! In *The Power of Habit*, Charles Duhigg adds that it takes at least 62 days to begin to sustain a lifelong habit. All this to say, you won't create a new habit or establish a new you overnight. It takes time.

We've talked about how easy it is to form regular habits growing up, but why is it so hard to stick with a new habit now? The main reason is that your brain is fighting itself. When you create a new habit, it requires two parts of the brain to work together: the prefrontal cortex and the basal ganglia.

The prefrontal cortex is the main manager of the brain and understands long-term benefits. It recognizes that eating healthy food now leads to a healthier body in the long run, or the need to save money helps build toward the goal of buying a new car. Essentially, your prefrontal cortex sees the potential in what could be and is constantly looking for efficient ways to reach those opportunities. With all those potentials swirling around in your head, it tends to take a toll on your energy, which leads to brain fatigue. The more you activate thoughts through your prefrontal cortex, the more likely you are to stumble and make poor decisions. This is also known as decision fatigue. You see, the prefrontal cortex is an energy hog that burns through blood glucose rapidly when engaging in new tasks. At the same time, it is working to recognize patterns to streamline this task if it's ever done again. Once your prefrontal cortex detects a pattern, it sends it to the basal ganglia and stores it as a neural pathway or synapsis. The basal ganglia holds immense stamina and saves energy by repeating habits that are stored there.

When we attempt to do anything new, the prefrontal cortex fires up and thinks, "How can this be done simpler and easier?" As you continue a habit, your basal ganglia automatically streamlines the task, and soon enough, it becomes a regular action in your life.

Much like the habit of driving a car or brushing your teeth, your prefrontal cortex passes the baton to your basal ganglia and lets it handle the controls. This is when the behavior that was once new (like learning to drive) becomes an auto-pilot response (like your commute to work).

KEYSTONE HABITS

A keystone habit creates a ripple effect throughout your day and your life. It could be something as simple as journaling when you first wake up, working out during your lunch break, or setting your phone aside before you go to bed. The action of doing this one thing positively impacts everything else in your day to feel more in flow. Take a look at your list of habits again and ask yourself, what particular habits positively influence your day the most?

In a study[1] that looked at two groups of people desiring to lose weight, the first control group was given no instructions, but the second group was told to record everything they ate. After six months, the group that wrote their food intake down was the group that began regularly modifying their eating, drinking, sleeping, and exercise habits for an increase in weight loss. Meanwhile, the control group without instruction stayed relatively at the same weight.

Writing down food intake is the perfect example of a keystone habit. For participants in the study, they became more aware of their eating patterns and more conscious of how to modify them. Writing down your food intake is a great example of a 1° Shift that will build upon itself over time. In looking at your habits list, take some time to distinguish any keystone habits— anything that appears to have a compounded return. Ask yourself, what are some keystone habits that you can shift into? Consider what new habits will make the biggest impact on your life over the next year. What is one thing you can do now to shift your habits toward the life you most want to live?

---

1. L. P. Svetkey et al., "Comparison of Strategies for Sustaining Weight Loss, the Weight Loss Maintenance Randomized Controlled Trial," JAMA 299 (2008): 1139-48

9

THE SCIENCE BEHIND A HABIT

"We first make our habits, and then our habits make us."
~ John Dryden

In the 1890s, a Russian physiologist named Ivan Pavlov stumbled upon the concept of classical conditioning by accident. When it came to feeding dogs in his laboratory, he noticed they would start salivating at the sight of food. He ran a series of experiments to see if he could further manipulate their behavior. He was able to successfully trigger the same salivating response in the dogs through any association with food, such as a lab assistant entering the room or by ringing a bell before the food came. Essentially, he had triggered a conditioned response that formed into a regular habit.

Much like Pavlov and his dogs, you can condition your brain to begin a new habit and stick to it. I have seen the same conditioned behavior occur with my goldfish, who became used to swimming around in circles whenever I picked up the fish food container. The goldfish only behaved this way when it saw my hand reach for the food container, and it knew it was time to eat.

This type of conditioning is not limited to animals. I was in the Marine Corps for a number of years, and I can promise you that not everyone was initially inclined to get up before dawn. You didn't have to be a part of the platoon for very long to learn to immediately get up when the drill instructor opened the door. By the end of boot camp, you would be popping out of bed on cue as soon as the drill instructor entered the room. This is an example of how we can create habits that steer us toward the life we want to lead.

A paper published by a Duke University researcher[1] in 2006 found that more than 40% of the actions we take each day are not decisions, but habits. If you're anything like me, you might do the same thing every day when you wake up. The first thing I do when I awake is to meditate and journal for about five minutes each. Then, I brush my teeth, get dressed, and head downstairs to take the dog out for a walk. As soon as I get back from the walk, I take off my shoes and head straight to turn on the coffee maker. It is the same routine for me every morning. It's my habit! On the rare occasion when I do something different, even my dog is confused about what the day is going to look like. It feels strange to get knocked out of my regular habit loop.

WHAT IS THE HABIT LOOP?

Why does it feel so hard for us to shift out of our habits? Why can't we easily implement a new routine that helps us, rather than an old one that doesn't? It's because we have habit loops running in the backgrounds of our lives.

Experts have defined habit loops in various ways, but one way of looking at it is how it is stored in the basal ganglia. It's a series of neural pathways or stored messages to be carried out upon the triggering of an initial cue.

A true habit loop includes the following elements:

Cue | Craving | Routine | Reward | Result

The loop has three phases. The first phase of the loop is the "problem phase" that involves the cue and craving aspects. The second phase of the habit loop is the "solution phase," where routine and reward live. The third phase is the "result phase," where the other two phases and the long term effects of the habit can be seen.

As you enter the loop, you're triggered by a cue in your brain and body. It could be something as simple as the feeling you get when you're thirsty. Throughout your day, you'll experience many cues, such as your stomach growling, the dog whining at the door, or your eyelids begin to droop down at a late hour. Your body gives an indication of what you need to do next in order to feel better, which leads you to the craving part of the habit loop. A great example of craving arises with digital clutter. As you're going to the kitchen with a particular task in mind, you hear your phone across the room ding, alerting you to a new notification. Immediately, you walk over to your phone to figure out what the notification is, and eventually, this becomes a conditioned habit. Every time your phone dings with a notification, you respond by checking it, despite what you were initially doing. This leads us to the routine part of the habit loop.

Following a routine can be great, but what happens after the routine? When you complete a task on your list for the day, how do you feel? Routines end with a sense of accomplishment that rewards us for our habit. Rewards can range from a non-tangible feeling to an actual physical reward that you've worked into your routine.

The completion of the habit loop is often overlooked, and it comes in the form of a result. A result can carry short-term and long-term benefits. Over time, we see results revealing themselves in our daily lives, such as hitting snooze only once rather than 10 times before getting up; eating healthy and feeling the difference in your body; or breaking the habit of checking your phone every time you get a notification. The results of established habits can take effect or trickle across nearly every aspect of your life, from the quality of your relationships to the wealth in your bank account or even the way your clothes fit. Every habit loop, from cue to result, leads to positive or negative feelings as an end response. You may be feeling proud of yourself, but some habits can also lead to the feeling of disappointment.

This is where the 1° Shift Method comes into play. When you look at your life, what changes feel natural? What changes are you trying to intentionally create? You are in control of consciously creating lasting results. Remember, the 1° Shift is a commitment to one small shift in emotion, thought, or action. We will dive even more into this in the chapters to come, and you'll soon be able to recognize habit loops that you've been living in. This will help you to initiate 1° Shifts seamlessly into your life.

NEURAL PATHWAYS

We've discussed the science behind habits, how habit loops are created, and how we associate them with certain results, but let's dive a little further into how to rewire habits to create your 1° Shift. Do you remember talking about the basal ganglia? We already know it is powerful, but it reaches its full potential when you learn how to work alongside it, rather than against it.

I first discovered all of this back in 2004 when I suffered my first full-blown panic attack. I was driving with my ex-grand-mother-in-law, her two dogs, and my two kids, when suddenly, I experienced tunnel vision. I pulled over to the side of the road and had my first panic attack right there with everyone in the car. I showed up at the Veteran's Hospital in tears having no clue what was wrong with me. After an assessment, they prescribed Prozac and another medication that made me feel like a zombie. It wasn't too long before the side effects of the medications began to show. My hair started falling out, but still, the doctors wanted me to stay on the medication for fear of another panic attack. I couldn't do it anymore.

I began to research panic attacks and anxiety, trying to find an answer to what was wrong with me, and how to address the root issues creating it. What I found in my search was shocking. Study after study revealed that panic attacks and anxiety are learned behaviors. I thought to myself, how could all of this be merely a learned behavior?

When we experience anxiety and have an initial attack, we begin to fear another attack happening. This, in turn, causes the next one to occur. The brain soon recognizes the pattern and keeps repeating it. Meanwhile, we continue to live in fear until the next one happens. Recall the habit loop? This is one of them.

After learning this, I was determined to break the cycle. I continued in my research and came across a book titled *Choice Theory* by William Glasser, M.D. Glasser argues that you get to choose your emotions. At first, I thought this was complete bullshit because I did not *choose* to have a panic attack. In turn, I also chose not to finish reading that book. However, *in Destructive Emotions, A Scientific Dialogue with the Dalai Lama*, I learned that changing your emotions and feelings breaks your regular neuropathways to create new ones. This answer helped me come to understand how and why my panic attacks were occurring.

Imagine for a moment that you are five years old. One day, you come home from school and accidentally let a bad word you heard from a classmate slip. Immediately, your sibling reacts and smacks you across the face. You're left with the stinging feeling of being hurt and confused. The prefrontal cortex and basal ganglia have not seen this happen before, so it looks for a pattern. Your brain makes a note of the behavior that causes your sibling to get upset and react.

Fast forward the timeline to high school. This time, you're standing outside the school in a heated argument with your significant other, who then smacks you across the face. You feel the same hurt and confusion. The brain remembers getting smacked as a child, and in turn, reacts the same way. This is a neural pathway getting stronger.

Continue down the timeline to college. The same scenario happens with a new acquaintance who also smacks you across the face. The same feeling of hurt and confusion runs deeper as the neural pathway becomes even stronger.

A few months later, you're out hiking with a friend in the wilderness. You're caught up in your thoughts and the beautiful surroundings that you don't see the tree branch swinging back to smack you square in the face. Bam! Immediately, you feel a familiar sense of hurt and confusion. You think, *wait a minute, why do I feel like this?* The smack in the face was the cue for your brain to trigger the neural pathway to feel the same feelings you did as a kid. This is how neural pathways are formed deeper over time. The more it happens, the stronger it becomes, and soon enough, that feeling becomes automatic. The neural pathway loop is created rather quickly.

The stimulus (or cue) is the smack across the face, leading to neural pathways that create a habitual response of sadness and confusion. Your brain has been trained and automatically responds a certain way, but the brain doesn't always recognize the source of this. In turn, over the years, you create coping mechanisms that provide a temporary fix (pouring that third glass of wine, eating that pint of ice cream, reaching out to an ex), and eventually, these habits lead to more destructive behaviors that can steer a person away from the life they want.

This example of being smacked across the face was constructed for illustrative purposes. It's important to realize that whether such incidents are normal or abnormal behavior in someone's life, neural pathways can be formed quickly with lasting effect.

BREAKING HABITS

Rewriting the story of your neural pathways takes time. At first, it can feel challenging to recognize what is happening and why you are reacting a certain way. With practice, you'll realize what is happening when repeated situations arise.

The first step in rewriting your neural pathways is to recognize what is going on in the first place and then to learn how to respond. The Dalai Lama teaches how you can break a habit by understanding that there is a split second from the time the cue happens to the triggered reaction. Once you recognize the cue, you can consciously choose to respond differently in the moment the synapsis is firing in your brain or in that split-second time frame. The key is to interrupt your regular pattern before it takes over and becomes an unconscious routine. It takes practice, but once you can break the pattern, you can control how you show up in life.

Take a moment to picture yourself sitting outside on the back porch. Suddenly, a mosquito lands on your arm. Your initial instinct is to smack it or wave it away from your arm to avoid getting bitten. This is an automatic response based on previous experience. But what if you watched it land on you, recognized your initial instinct to smack it, and didn't. You let it bite you and fly away.

Your regular pattern kicks in your neural pathway the moment you have the urge to smack the mosquito, but you shift your pattern by watching it fly away. You've stepped into that split second, and you've refrained from your usual behavior. This isn't about the mosquito buzzing around you—it's about how you react—whether it feels automatic or is a conscious choice. This applies to every situation we are faced with that triggers our automatic response and how we can step outside the pattern to make a different choice. You're shifting behavior from a reaction to a response. A response implies control, you are consciously choosing to respond and create a different habit, like setting out a citronella candle before you sit outside to keep mosquitos away. That is both a choice and a proactive response.

Our problem is our reactionary habits. When your phone buzzes, you immediately check it. When someone asks you to do something, you reactively say "yes". When you feel hungry, your first reaction is to grab a snack. All of these reactions are done quickly with little thought. Instead of letting your auto-response drive for you, you can look internally to be mindful of what you want to be doing instead of your routine response.

This behavior is called a "pattern interrupt." It is exactly what you think it is. You break the pattern. You respond purpose-fully instead of letting your brain react for you.

After my first panic attack, I realized I needed to listen to my intuition and take responsibility for my own life. I was constantly reacting, rather than responding. With practice, I began to figure out what triggered my anxiety. My triggers included lack of sleep, period cramps, too much caffeine, and certain types of alcohol. I learned to respond differently the next time the situation presented itself. I rewired my neural pathways simply by interrupting my habits.

One way to interrupt the pattern can be to name the things you see. "I see a mug on the table, a plant in the corner, a chair at the table, a cat on the couch." This pulls you into the present moment and kicks you out of the loop. Speaking out loud to the room pulls your senses along with it to see, hear, smell, and voice what is in the room. As a coach, I have applied this with many PTSD clients with whom I work. When they experience flashbacks of a traumatic event, I encourage them to recognize the loop beginning and to choose to respond differently. The development of presence and ownership of choice interrupts the regular pattern and creates a different ending.

When you notice a trigger, give yourself permission to inter-rupt the pattern without judgment. How do you want to feel at this moment? What is in alignment with your best self? Another approach to this is to express gratitude. Tell yourself, *"I am grateful I am no longer in that situation. I am safe. I am cared for."* It can be easy to fall back into the pattern of negative thoughts, but breaking the loop requires you to see a different way out—one that comes from a positive outlook.

By practicing this when you are triggered, your brain will begin to reframe its response. Over time, you will create a thoughtful, positive response. One client reached out to me expressing how much this had helped her, and I could not help but feel immense gratitude in the moment because I had gone through a similar experience myself.

Interrupting the pattern is a wonderful tool for creating the life you want. Take a moment to identify the habit loops in your life. What are your cues? What are your triggers? It could be something as simple as seeing a piece of cake that sets off a chain reaction of binge eating. It could be hitting snooze multiple times and showing up late to work. Write down different ways you can respond to bad habits, internally and externally. Don't forget to be kind to yourself—interrupting the pattern takes time.

ONE HABIT AT A TIME

Many people ask the question if they can shift two habits at once. While it might sound simple to do so, studies reveal that creating neural pathways to break the pattern is more effective when you focus on only one habit at a time.

When people try to learn a new skill, it takes them three times as long as when they are attempting multiple skills at once. This is true for people in all age groups. We can avoid this mental block by creating a new habit in-between two established habits. This is called habit sandwiching, or habit stacking. Capitalizing on your established habits helps conserve energy while creating a healthy new habit.

Remember, new lessons can feel exhausting for the brain. This is why your basal ganglia stores patterns for you. Focus on one new habit at a time. When you feel you've mastered it and see it positively affect other aspects of your life, then you can take another look at your list and start shifting into a new habit.

At this point, you may be wondering, *where do I begin to shift my habits?* Take a deep breath and exhale. Then, get your notebook and establish a plan for the following:

1. Decide what you want to change in your life.
2. Look at your current habits and ask yourself, "Can I

sandwich this new habit in between two existing habits?" **Current Habit | New Habit | Current Habit**

3. Commit to cultivating this new habit for a minimum of 3 months.

4. Find a buddy to keep you accountable. Success is much more attainable when you have someone else looking out for your best interests too.

Shifting into focused habit development can create a quick boost within your life and help you craft the life you most desire.

Remember, new lessons or tasks can feel exhausting for the brain. This is why the prefrontal cortex sends these new patterns to the basal ganglia to store them for later. As my coach Andrea says, "Movement creates momentum." These small shifts create momentum quickly.

---

1. "Habits - A repeat Performance" Current Directions in Psychological Science 15, no. 4 (2006): 198-202.

10

WILLPOWER & HABITS

"Motivation is what gets you started. Habit is what keeps you going."

~ Jim Ryun

*W*alter Mischell and his team at the Stanford Bing Nursery ran a revolutionary willpower exercise known as "The Marshmallow Experiment." Researchers gave each kid a plate with one marshmallow on it. Before leaving the room, they told the kid they could either eat the marshmallow immediately, or they can wait 15 minutes and get two marshmallows. While some of the kids ate the marshmallow immediately, most waited a few minutes before eating it (some nibbled at it slowly). A few rare kids patiently waited the entire 15 minutes and were rewarded with a second marshmallow. Years later, researchers discovered that the same kids who waited the 15 minutes had better test scores, were more popular among peers, participated in more activities, and were more involved in the community.

This study raises an interesting question, why do some people have more willpower than others? Can it be taught, or is it

ingrained? Before we dive into this, let's look at what influences willpower.

7 KEY FACTORS THAT DEPLETE WILLPOWER

- Effort
- Perceived Difficulty
- Negative Effect
- Subjective Fatigue
- Blood Glucose Levels
- Stress
- Decision Fatigue

1. Effort

Effort is straightforward. You try, or you don't. The more effort
and time we give toward change, the more we feel accomplished as a result.

2. Perceived Difficulty

Perceived difficulty often holds us back the most. An example
of this can be found when implementing a new exercise
routine. The first day you feel motivated and get in a great
workout. This feels awesome. The next day you may just not
feel up to it, and by the time the sun has set, you've already
talked yourself out of it before even starting.

3. The Negative Effect

The negative effect is a learned behavior where you've
attempted something in the past, and it went horribly wrong.
Prior negative experience keeps you from even attempting
something again out of fear it will turn out the same way.

4. Subjective Fatigue

Subjective fatigue is an external factor. It could be anything from a draining toxic friendship to a poor work environment to an unhealthy family dynamic.

5. Blood Glucose Levels

A lack of glucose in your system depletes your energy and hinders your ability to make rational decisions.

6. Stress

Stress impacts your mental, physical, and emotional wellbeing. A high-stress lifestyle can damage your energy levels and leave little room for you to focus on what you actually want to do.

7. Decision Fatigue

Our decision-making abilities deteriorate as the day progresses. Decision fatigue is created when we are forced to make decisions with depleted energy. This can affect our motivation to achieve what we said we would do.

Willpower is closely linked to creating the life you want. Something always comes up when we desire to interrupt our regular patterns. We procrastinate and put excuses in front of change and pair these with low levels of motivation. Like the habit of immediately checking your phone, it takes time to train your willpower to kick in so that you can shift the pattern you're used to living in. It takes willpower to resist the urge to look at or respond to your device when you have other priorities with which to contend.

This relates back to a technique we've discussed previously—planning your day. Take a look back at the Four Quadrants in Chapter 3. This is the first major step in the right direction. If you can muster the willpower to shift a habit, your prefrontal cortex will align, knowing there is a long-term benefit involved. Presence of mind will help by telling your basal ganglia to memorize the pattern. Whether you want money, peace of mind, or stronger relationships, it takes willpower to commit to change, and the best avenue of pursuit is shifting 1° at a time.

THE CLARITY EXERCISE

This is where the clarity exercise can help us establish our priorities when we experience factors that deplete our willpower.

1. What is my intention?

Intention starts with an objective. If you want to be healthier, what does that look like in smaller steps? It could be incorporating more fruit and vegetables in your diet, working out 30 minutes a day, or joining a fitness class. By identifying your intention, you can create smaller steps toward reaching your objective.

2. What obstacles are in my way?

What obstacles are keeping you from reaching your goal? Your busy schedule? Continually hitting snooze and waking up later? Constant low energy from stress? Take a moment to write down your objective, intention, and everything that is keeping you from success.

Once you've discovered these, it's time to plan how to break old habits and form positive, new ones. Start your day with your intention rather than creating excuses for yourself. Think about the ways you can reach your objective every single day. Whether it's grocery shopping for different foods rather than getting fast food or taking 30 minutes before work to exercise, you have to correlate your intention to your action. Remember, it only takes a very small shift in your day to make a big impact.

In 1992,[1] British psychologists Sheina Orbell and Paschal Sheeran looked at the correlation between planning and recovery rates for patients with hip replacements who were 60 years of age or older. They divided the patients into two groups. The first group was given a rehabilitation booklet and sent out with guidelines to recover on their own. The second group was given the same booklet, but this time, the booklet had blank pages and instructions to write down their plan of action after reading each section. The results of the study showed that the group with a set plan of action recovered twice as fast as the group who were just told to read the booklet and learn on their own. This shows how writing down a plan of action drives real results.

RESISTANCE & REWARD

After undergoing spinal fusion surgery on my L4/L5 vertebrae, I rarely exercised outside of the daily walk or hike. Eventually, after 2 full years, I felt inspired to take Kino MacGregor's 30-day yoga challenge on YouTube. I did some research, found a new yoga mat, and committed to the challenge. Some days felt easy, while other days I struggled to find the motivation to get through it. Over the course of the challenge, my arms felt tighter, my back was stronger, and I was even sleeping better! I was riding high with my achievement, but it wasn't long after the challenge was over that I fell back into old habits. I no longer had a formula to follow toward my intention, and as a result, I experienced every level of willpower depletion.

We've all fallen after achieving a high. Just think of how many people you know who lost weight, only to gain it back after their motivation was gone. When there is seemingly no more need for this newfound habit, it's easy to slip back into old patterns. Essentially, those old habits are lying dormant in your basal ganglia, just waiting to re-emerge. Your prefrontal cortex is doing everything it can to fire all cylinders for a new habit, but that, in turn, depletes your energy resources, forcing you to tiredly return to old habits. This is where emotions become involved, and we feel disappointed about our lack of progress. Once your routine implants itself within your basal ganglia, your neural pathways begin to become stronger and better able to support the life you are pursuing.

This is the same reason New Year's resolutions fail. We promise we will go to the gym every day, but after three weeks, we've already turned back to old habits of binge-watching shows after work or something of the sort. The greatly anticipated "reward" suddenly becomes less exciting.

This is where the habit loop comes into play. You're working on creating a new habit loop, you've done all the steps, but it is ultimately your willpower that has to kick in and make it happen. When you feel close to achieving a reward, pause for a moment, and think *how do I feel in this moment?* That feeling of achievement encourages the positive habit loop to stick and continue leading you to lasting results.

When developing a new routine, oftentimes, a "partial rein-forcement extinction effect" can occur, which means you are not getting the result you thought you would when repeating the same action every time. It can feel discouraging when you're not making the progress you anticipate, but this is where you can spice it up a little. Think about a fitness goal. Instead of repeating the same exercises every day and listening to the same music, change it up. You still have your eyes on the result, but you're staying fresh to keep your mind and body motivated. So, go ahead and find new music to listen to, change up your workout clothes, and find something you feel confident in. Whatever your goal is, you're more likely to achieve your intention through seeking different and creative ways to reach the same result.

Document an action plan to reinforce your commitment to creating this new habit. Create a ritual around your new habit. That might involve doing it at the same time every day, if possible. Focus on progress and not perfection. Don't rush. There are going to be days when you go above and beyond your habit, and days when you can only do the minimum, but at this stage, the most important thing is that you are doing something to help create that new habit. Don't try to move too quickly. Habits take time to create, but you will find yourself improving. Be happy with all of your progress. This positivity will help you begin to crave the reward through the positive results it's creating in your life.

Once we become more aware of our habits, triggers, and how the brain works to form new routines, it's natural to want to try and fix everything immediately. Relax. Be Patient. Keep track of everything you want to change, but maintain your focus on the bigger picture.

Creating new habits can be challenging. If you find a habit buddy, you are more likely to achieve your goal, so don't hesitate to team up with a friend or family member. You might be surprised to find more people willing to join you than you think. We're all tired of dealing with the bullshit alone. We have to be responsible for ourselves, but that doesn't mean we can't help or seek help from others who are in a similar boat. We aren't meant to do everything alone. We are truly meant to be part of a tribe. Be encouraged to seek peace, comfort, and grace in relationships.

---

1. Orbell, Sheina & Sheeran, Paschal. (2006). Motivational and Volitional Processes in Action Initiation: A Field Study of the Role of Implementation Intentions1. Journal of Applied Social Psychology. 30. 780 - 797.

PART IV
YOUR VISION

11

YOUR DREAM LIFE

"Find out who you are and do it on purpose."
~ Dolly Parton

At this point, you've explored many aspects of your life. You've written down your habits, what priorities you want to focus on, how to declutter your life, and how to establish better boundaries. You've dabbled in the power of habits and explored the concept of established routine.

Now it's time to look at vision, and not just any vision—*your vision*. Having a clear vision will allow you to know exactly where you are going, and when you plan to get there. When we understand where we are going, we are better equipped to make clear shifts toward achievement.

This exercise can help you begin to establish true vision for your life.

Question #1: What is my current reality?

Where are you at right now? What does your life look like, feel like, etc. Don't censor yourself or write for anybody else. This is for you. Pull your notebook out again and free-write every-thing that feels hard, what comes easy, and what is good or bad in your current reality. Let it flow.

Question #2: How do I feel about where I'm at? Why do I feel this way?

The more honest you can be here, the closer you are to reaching your true vision. Find the cracks you often fall into, what holds you back, and what interactions make you feel a particular way. This can relate to your personal life, relation-ships, or work—whatever is affecting you at this moment. Be as specific as possible.

Question #3: What is my dream life?

If you could have anything in the world, what would it be? How would your life look? Be specific! Include everything from the type of people you want to hang around to your occu-pation, to the foods you eat, to your daily routine.

I recommend that you take your time on this exercise and consider devoting an entire page to each aspect of your life: work, health, friends, house, etc. The more you can sit with your thoughts and your vision for the future, the more acces-sible this future becomes.

IS THIS YOUR DREAM?

Okay, you've written down your ultimate "dream life." Now what? This is where we find the truth in what you desire. At times, we think we have an idea for what we want, only to discover later that it really isn't what we truly wanted. It turns out it was only what we *thought* we wanted and not what we *actually* wanted.

Many years ago, I worked as a spiritual coach at a local new age center. The head of the center held weekly enrichment classes for all employees. During one of our peer-led classes, we were asked to write down our dream life. We then shared with everyone else what we had written down.

At the time, I had this image in my head of owning a massive house on a large piece of property with all the things you could imagine that went with it. When I shared my dream life with the group, it always circled back to the big house. But when I shared this vision with the group, I could feel my energy drop. The head of the center immediately noticed and asked, "What's going on there?"

"This feels heavy. I don't want to clean a giant house like that," I told her.

My dream house suddenly felt hard and burdensome. Speaking my vision out loud revealed this wasn't actually how my version of what success looked. It wasn't my true vision of ease, flow, abundance, and wealth. I had to take a few steps back and ask myself, *"What is my dream life? What do I actually want?"*

I had to redefine how this looked to me. My original vision had become stale and outdated in what I desired for my life. I remember closing my eyes, focusing on my heart space, and slowing my breathing. I searched for what felt easy, calm— what felt like a sacred sanctuary. I recognized that what I wanted wasn't a large house full of things. What I truly desired was a smaller home with lots of windows I could look out. A home that felt spacious, yet cozy. My vision began to pour out of me, and I wrote down pages and pages of everything I wanted. I envisioned the friends with whom I'd surround myself, how I would look after my wellbeing, how I would take care of my family, and more.

Your task now is to go back to what you wrote down as your dream life and ask yourself, *"Does this line up with my definition of ease, comfort, and flow?"* If not, how can this dream life become even more specific to what you truly desire? This is an important exercise, as what you write for your dream life is your roadmap, and without it, you'll walk down paths that aren't truly leading to the life you ultimately seek.

LIVING A LIFE OF EASE & OPPORTUNITY

Deep down, we all want to live a life that exudes ease. We grew up with the mentality that we have to "work hard" to get what we want in life. But what if there was an easier way? What if life didn't have to be so hard?

What blocks most people in this part is the issue of defining clearly what feels easy and aligned for them. What comes easy for one person isn't necessarily easy for someone else. Let's try to define what this looks like.

Answer these four questions:

1. What does "ease" look like for me?
2. Have I ever experienced ease and flow? If yes, when?
3. Who do I know that lives a life of ease?
4. What are those people doing differently than me?

My sons seem to move through life with ease and flow. If they want something, they manifest it into their lives. They claim to have learned this from me, but they both are much more graceful than I am when it comes to pursuing their happiness. It is incredible to watch them manifest so fluidly.

What can you learn from those who live and manifest with ease and flow? My kids don't just trust in what they want in life, they believe without a doubt that they will receive it. They know that the Universe will provide for their desires. They don't hope or wait—they believe! When you desire something, know that you are more than ready to receive it.

We all have had experiences that hold us in challenging places, which can make it feel impossible to move forward. Consider what holds you in place where you're at right now. Instead of focusing negatively on those things that hold you back, let's shift and find the opportunities.

Let's look at something many people suffer from: Money. When someone is in debt, there is a ton of stress around basics, such as bills and living expenses. Let's look at debt. If you pay late or not at all, it hurts your credit score and wracks up even more debt. How can you break the cycle for this? You must look for solutions. Inquire about payment plans that have minimal damage or penalties. Begin to shift your spending habits. Declutter and sell items to bring in extra cash. Pick up an extra shift at work. Start a side business. Look for every possible avenue toward getting out of debt. Even just writing out a plan for this helps to shift your mindset around money. In turn, you're clearing the clutter in your head and removing negative cycles from your life. Such 1° Shifts will affect everything else moving forward.

How can you shift a roadblock into an opportunity? Simple. You must shift your perspective. Take time to look at a particular situation from the following four perspectives.

1. What You Tell Yourself

How do you talk to yourself throughout the day? Do you speak positively? Do you beat yourself up with negative "what ifs?" Consider how you can empower yourself to a new level.

I once had a client who would say, "I'm so stupid! I can't believe I did this again. I'm never going to learn!" After hearing this week after week, I asked her to reflect on her dominant thoughts throughout the day and her self-talk. She was shocked at what she discovered. These types of thoughts are often unconscious ways we keep ourselves stuck by programing our thoughts for limitation through repeated negative mantras.

2. How You Feel—aka Your Energy

Just like Mother Nature's four seasons, we too move through seasons. Through winter, we have low energy and feel like hibernating. When spring comes, we have more energy and tend to be focus-driven. As summer comes, we are generally more chill and our energy is neutral until autumn rolls around, and we become more determined or task-focused.

Many of us over-schedule. We can't seem to cram everything we want to get done in a day and soon are frustrated with ourselves and everything around us. Remember that your energy is cyclical, just like the seasons. Some days are meant for hibernating, while others are meant for focused achievement. Instead of beating yourself up when you can't achieve everything, make a list of priorities. What can you get done today? What can wait until tomorrow? Most importantly, don't judge yourself if you have low energy days. Sit with yourself and move in flow.

3. Get Out Of The Pattern Of "Hard"

Are there patterns in your life that feel harder than others? Is it your long commute to work? A repeated argument in your relationship? A job you hate? While some things in life are just plain hard, we often make them worse through a negative mindset.

One of my clients wanted to reduce the amount of stress in her life. After talking for a while, she determined that her drive to work stressed her out the most. She had fallen into the habit of watching the news in the morning before determining which route to take to work. When looking at aspects contributing to commute stress, we found that the negatively charged energy of the news was affecting her mood in the morning. As a solution, I suggested she leave 15 minutes earlier, take the route she enjoyed more, and skip the news altogether. After a few weeks, she felt better in the mornings, and she significantly reduced her stress levels.

Humans are creatures of habit and routine, and because of this, we create rituals for our day to conserve energy. These rituals, or habits, start from a need or desire. When life shifts, we sometimes neglect modifying our routines or habits accordingly. This often causes us to continue doing things that no longer make our lives easier and instead, make them more difficult. Something that was once beneficial becomes burdensome.

The key is to be aware when a routine no longer serves us. That is the cue to break the pattern and shift your focus. My drive into the city can take forty-five minutes of high-stress driving if I take the direct route. If I shift my route to be a little bit longer, I end up driving through side streets with gorgeous lampposts and beautiful scenery. That little shift takes the stress out of driving and is a benefit of ease to my day.

This can relate to not only your morning routine but also things you immediately do when you get home and anything else that is a regular pattern for you. Pay attention to how you go about your day and work to identify the patterns that feel hard or cumbersome. Look for opportunities that allow you to shift and move in flow and ask yourself how things could feel easier.

4. Simplify Your Goals

Stephen R. Covey asks, "What's one thing, if done daily for one year, would make the biggest impact on your life?" We over-complicate our lives by spinning too many plates at once, only to watch them shatter on the floor in our own disappointment. I'm guilty of this too.

Several years ago, I decided to try something different. Instead of balancing 10 different aspects of my business, I focused on one—my Mastermind Mafia Program. This program was designed to help women build, grow, and scale their online coaching businesses to six figures. I had already worked with clients one-on-one in this way for years, but this time, I wanted it to be available to the masses.

Simplifying my focus to one goal was scary because I was used to balancing five or six different projects at once. For the first time in a long time, I was able to be present in my body and stay in the moment. It forced me to become crystal clear about everything that was non-essential to my business. Focusing on this one goal made everything else flow as it allowed me to not only expand my business but also serve more people.

What would your life look like if you chose to focus on one thing at a time? How would your relationships benefit? Your wellbeing? Allow yourself to embody and embolden this vision for your life through the idea of making 1° Shifts in the direction of your vision.

BELIEVING AS IF…

For us to get the life we want and to allow it to feel the way we desire, we need to believe it is truly possible. Let's look at what already feels easy and in-flow to you right now. Is it loving your kids? Sleeping in? Driving your car? Loving your partner?

As you hold onto this feeling of ease, ask yourself, "What if every aspect of my life could feel like this? How would I feel? How would I act? How would I start and end every day? Would this change the way I show up for myself and others?"

Who could you be if you embodied the definition of ease?

Many times, when presented a new opportunity to create or have something new, we instantly feel an energy boost, get excited, and can't wait to get started. Then, our old thought habits come swooping in and remind us of our current status. Our mind starts convincing ourselves why we need to stay in our comfort zone and be content with what we have. We may feel a mixture of excitement and fear. Excitement for what we could have and fear that we may not get it.

Remember earlier in the book we talked about how fear and excitement feel the same in the physical body, yet also feel entirely different energetically? Fear is tight, restrictive, and heavy. Excitement feels open, expansive, and free. Allow yourself to feel the freedom of opportunity—even for these few moments.

If you want to bring something new into your life, you have to begin that 1° Shift toward that new thing you want. It's not as simple as just doing it—it is believing as if it can truly happen. Allow yourself to embody the energy if its completion. In doing so you hone clarity of thought and gain the courage to take the first step. It's also confidence. You must add confidence to the choices you are prepared to make. Be confident in yourself and the ownership you are taking in your life. Remind yourself regularly that you have a right to make decisions in your own life. You are not victim to your circumstances, and you have more control over your life than anyone else does.

Take a moment to focus on what type of mindset you want to have while you are creating these shifts in your life. How would it feel to live in the home of your dreams? How would it feel to be debt-free? Now think, what do you need to reach those feelings? When you tie your feelings directly to your vision and then implement courageous action with confidence, you set yourself up for attainment.

In the next few chapters, we will look at mindset, spiritual laws, intuition, and how each of these will help you to implement tiny 1° Shifts in your life. It's time to pursue the life you envision.

12

MINDSET AND DOMINANT THOUGHTS

"Whether you think you can, or think you can't, you're right."
~ Henry Ford

*W*hen I first read this quote, it changed the trajectory of my life. When you think you can, doors open, and everything just falls into place. When you think you can't, things go wrong. You are in control of what you say, what you do, and what you think. Naturally, though, this may be met with resistance. There will be times where your brain fights back and comes up with every excuse to convince you to just stop trying. These are ways your brain tries to conserve energy and also keeps you in your comfort zone.

For instance, if you want to be an artist, you may hear over and over again that artists never make any money, and you should just get a real job already. Belief in that statement equates to bullshit that spins excuses through every aspect of your life. I know plenty of artists who make enough money to support themselves and their family simply by sharing their gifts with the world. Perhaps you want to be a coach, but your mind tells you to be more realistic. Another bullshit excuse. You have to leave the excuses at the door.

Recognize the chatter in your head for what it is—voices that hold you back from what you really want. If you don't let go of the excuses you create, you will be stuck where you are indefinitely. You might be thinking by now, *"No Flora, I really wanted this thing in my life. I believed that I could get it, but then this whole shit storm happened and now it's just not realistic."* When we begin to change our thoughts, we may begin to notice qualifiers or disclaimers running through our heads. These are reasons why or why not we can or cannot have something.

Imagine you own your own business, and you want to bring in $20,000 this month. Your normal monthly revenue is $15,000. You may be very comfortable at the $15,000 a month mark, but thinking about bringing in $20,000 may trigger a host of dominant thoughts that begin to tell you why you can't reach your new goal.

"Sure, my business can bring in $20,000 this month," but in the back of your mind, you really are thinking, *"I'm going to have to work twice as long".* Thoughts like this derail your beliefs and sidetrack your vision.

Knowing your intention is just half the battle. You have to meet the Universe halfway by believing without a doubt that you can create the life you want. I see many people try and fail because they assume they aren't meant to do what they desire, and this belief dominates their thoughts. When you encounter this type of resistance, you must shift your plan, not your goal.

Look at different ways of approaching your intention and break down creative ways of how to get there. My previous book, "Year in Reverse," addresses this through the approach of reverse-engineering your goals into bite-sized steps, allowing you to achieve anything you put your mind to.

Look at where you are now. Compare it to where you want to be. What are the stepping stones that bridge that gap? If you're making $500 a month, but your goal is to make $20,000, reel it back in and set your steps to gradually increase. Start with $1,000, then move to $2,000. It takes little steps for big intention to find its way. What you may not realize is that we do this type of thinking every day with little awareness of even doing so.

Think of what you were like as a child. Children want all types of things and have no problem rattling off their wish list. As you get older, you tend to censor your thoughts and focus more on what you need, rather than what you want. Don't be afraid to shift your energy and look at what you desire. Allow the energy that is born from desire to manifest itself into your life.

Let's put this into perspective. Imagine, you've moved into a brand-new apartment. In the evening as it is getting dark, you realize you will need to get a lamp because the overhead light simply won't do. As a quick response, you drive to the store, buy a lamp, and set it up in your new apartment. You made it happen. You manifested that lamp. You might be thinking, *"Well, not really. I bought that lamp."* True, but you had the desire for more light, and you made it happen. That thought became a real action.

From a different perspective, you might not have had enough money for a lamp, but you still had the same desire for one. Same scenario. You thought about how you need more light in your apartment. Then at work, you overhear a colleague who is giving away household items before they move. They happen to have a lamp! Although you didn't have the funds, the Universe or God conspired on your behalf and found another way.

The process in which we manifest wants, needs, and goals are all one in the same. What you desire, whether it's for your highest good or not, starts to manifest for you. You must leverage your intentions and desires. Don't underestimate the power of the mind.

WHAT DO YOU FEED YOUR MIND?

Everything you do starts with a thought that can free you or imprison you. Many of us get stuck in thought loops, thinking the same thoughts over and over again. These thoughts keep us stuck where we are, making it feel almost impossible to have, be, or do anything new. This happens when we don't challenge ourselves with new ideas. When you don't feed your mind new things, how could you possibly think differently?

Do you feed your mind sensationalized news or hyped-up social media articles? Negative stories spike our stress levels and contribute to our thoughts. The same goes for various forms to include movies, books, and gaming.

Think for a moment about how many of your thoughts in the day are devoted to your social circles. Who are the people you hang out with the most? We are a reflection of the five closest people to us, and their behaviors have a direct influence on what we think of ourselves (and the world around us). If your friends complain all the time, it's inevitable that you will complain, as well. When your friends strive for success, you too begin to look at your situation with a positive outlook and seek new solutions. We simply become a product of whatever environment we choose to live in. It all starts in your head and is compounded with what you choose to feed your mind. You have the ability to shift your life by feeding your mind with positive thoughts that lead toward the mindset you most desire.

SHIFTING YOUR MINDSET

The mind is strong, stubborn, and too often stuck in its ways, but you can use this to your advantage. For every way we inadvertently self-sabotage or stand in our own way, we also have the ability to do the opposite. We have the power to make our dreams become reality. Pay close attention to your intuition, identify triggers, and learn to understand why certain things cause you to feel or think a particular way. Then, find the path to replace your negative thought with a positive one.

Whether we realize it or not, our thoughts inspire action. Thinking creates movement toward a desire, but it can also block us from taking action. You might be thinking, *"How could I possibly determine whether a thought affects my life?"* Your life is a tangible result of how your thoughts and reflections influence everything around you. Your present situation is nothing more than the accumulation of your past thoughts and actions. Your bank account, your home, your health, your relationships —are all a result of your thoughts, which, in turn, lead to the actions you took to get where you are today.

We tend to think negative thoughts and point to bad luck. When I have clients in my coaching practice who claim they are on a string of bad luck, I suggest that they take a step back and look at a time they experienced good luck. What happened that was different from their bad luck?

It is often a job loss, breakup, betrayal, or hardship that has kicked them out of the happy zone and into a difficult period of life. It wasn't just the negative event that changed their luck, it was the fact they dwelled in it for an extended period. Over time, they fell into a downward spiral of which they had trouble getting out. As we will discuss in the next chapter, the "Law of Increase" brings us more of what we focus on, and this works both positively and negatively.

All of those old stories we keep in the back of our minds can become unconscious limitations that will continue to impede us. It gets to the point where you talk about the past so much that you slowly convince yourself that it will always be this way. With every thought you have, you are creating your future. You are co-creating your reality with the source of energy (God, Universe, Your Higher Power). You must believe that you can consciously create your future. Begin to envision what your deepest desires are and then be willing to take inspired action toward them.

The way that you think influences everything around you. Our desires influence our thoughts. Our thoughts impact the actions we take. I see clients read every book they can, listen to all the podcasts, take class after class, and have no results to show for anything. This is because we never took the time to put all those things we have learned into action.

You get to decide, today, that this is the beginning of the rest of your story. To consciously choose a life of intention. This is the day you get to apply the 1° Shift across every aspect of your life. Don't just think it, or believe it, choose to act on it.

13

TAKING YOUR POWER BACK

"The best way to predict the future is to create it!"
~ Stephen R. Covey

*H*ow can you shift out of autopilot and into creating what you want? Think about the people you know who somehow breeze their way through life while you're over in the corner freaking out. The real secret they hold is the way they think. Whether they realize it or not, they've trained their brain for ease. If you take a look at the most successful people in the world today, you will notice that they look for opportunities, rather than focus on the adversities they face. They are the type of people who look for a window when the door is closed. While in college, we studied Donald Trump and how he approaches business and everyday decision making. While he did inherit money from his father, he also filed for bankruptcy multiple times and somehow always managed to bounce back. One of the ways he achieves this is by scripting his day to what he believes to be true. He tells himself what he is going to do, what will happen, how things are in the moment, but more importantly, he convinces himself it is true.

He puts himself in a powerful mindset toward his view of success.

While attending a mastermind retreat in California, Peter Diamandis, author, engineer and founder of the X-Prize Foundation, spoke about confidence and reaching goals. During the discussion, he explained how every single morning he writes down what his day will look like. He manifests what he wants for his life. He calls it his "moonshot." He asks himself, *"What is something I want that people say can't be done?"* Not only does he try to achieve this, but he also takes inspired action to do so. His belief and daily mindset work together to make all the difference.

Most of us struggle to believe that something good will happen to us. We are so used to muscling through how we think, that we can't find another way of looking at it. At some point in our lives, it all becomes too much. We shift into autopilot, but what would it feel like to turn the autopilot off? To take back the controls? Stopping to think about how you're feeling helps you find a better sense of what you really want and what inspired action you need to take. Once you've learned to shift your mindset, you will realize that your dream life is much closer than you think.

One easy way to begin this is through the use of power phrases.

POWER PHRASES

The Strangest Secret by Earl Nightingale explains how when you write down what you want and repeat it over and over again, you can bring that desire into your life. This practice is mentioned in a number of my favorite go-to books: *Think and Grow Rich* by Napoleon Hill, *Write It Down, Make It Happen* by

Henriette Anne Klauser, and *Wake Up and Live* by Dorothea Brand, to name a few.

What are power phrases? They are affirmations that can help shift your mind to what you want to achieve. The key is to write out the phrase as if you already have it. It's as simple as telling yourself, *"I am focused throughout my day"*. If it becomes a regular message you tell yourself, over time, it shifts into something you do on a daily basis. You might be thinking, *"Okay, well, it couldn't possibly work with, 'I always have enough money' because that is out of my control!"* But this is not true. You are in control of your life *and* what you bring into it.

Here are a few examples of power phrases:

- I attract helpful people in my life and business.
- I have a supportive partner who listens and hears what I'm saying.
- I am a powerful steward of money.
- I am wise in my spending habits.
- I make the best food choices for my body.
- I have a fabulous fitness routine.
- I get paid to be me.
- I always have the perfect job for me.
- I am focused throughout my day.
- I am present with my partner and children.
- I honor my energy levels.
- I always drink enough water.
- I always have enough money for everything I need, want, or desire.
- I easily reach my goals.

Now, I have to be honest for a moment, mindset was not always something I believed in. In fact, I thought it was a load of bullshit. I grew up in an entrepreneurial family that hustled 24/7 to make ends meet. I thought if I spent enough hours working hard enough that I would get what I wanted. Needless to say, I was overworked, underpaid, and burnt out! I hired coach after coach, and each of them said the same thing, *"You've got everything right—you just have to work on your mindset!"*

After my third coach in a row told me this, I was angry but humbled. I then began researching the greats: Oprah, Tony Robbins, Napoleon Hill, Earl Nightingale. They all said that mindset influenced their success the most. They all focused on their dominant state of mind and discovered what they truly wanted. Anytime it wavered, they would shift their focus back to their intention.

When I started to play with mindset work and power phrases, I was a true skeptic. What made me a believer was my commitment to trying out a few power phrases for 30 days. *"I always have enough money"* was a power phrase I used when getting myself out of debt. I began saying it more and noticed that my mindset about debt began shifting. I became more mindful of how I spent my cash. I no longer used credit cards, and I was able to pay off my debts and save money too. I didn't become wealthier overnight, but I became aware of what I wanted, needed, and already had. Inevitably, we can't plan for everything, and the unexpected does come up, especially when you have kids. When you're aware of your finances, you can make sure to have enough money for everything you want, need, and desire. Write it down. Repeat it. Believe it. Embody it. It will become a part of you. In *7 Habits of Highly Effective People*, Stephen R. Covey says, *"The best way to predict the future is to create it."* And that's exactly what this is.

I also tried this method out when I was frequently arguing with one of my sons during his teenage years. I realized I was so focused on arguing that I just attracted more of it. Instead, I flipped the script and told myself, *"I always hear what my son is saying. I hear the meaning behind his words. I always understand what he is trying to say. My son always hears me, he hears the meaning behind my words, and he always understands me."* I repeated that over and over again. It wasn't long before we started to hear each other and stopped arguing. I just needed to shift my focus from the negative to the positive.

An important part of doing this is to recognize how you talk to yourself and the words you choose to use. For instance, you've paid off your debts and are basking in the glory of it, but suddenly, you find yourself back in debt. The whole time you were so focused on being in debt that your energy stayed in the debt zone. To change your energy frequency around money, you have to utilize power phrases that shift your focus to be more mindful of how you spend your money. One approach to doing this is to shift your focus work from "debt" to "investment." Let's say you owe $5,000 on a Target credit card. Every time you go to pay the bill, recognize that you have a good relationship with Target, so much so that the lending company provided money you needed to invest in the life you are currently living. Every time you pay another piece of your investment off, you pay into the system that helped you when you needed it. A simple mindset shift will change your energy in this space and work to heal your relationship with debt.

These questions and affirmations can help jumpstart your journey:

- What do I want today?
- What would feel good?
- Why do I want this?
- What would feel the best for me at this moment?
- How am I supported in my life (or in this moment)?
- What would feel fun?

- What else can I do to bring what I want into my life that feels exciting?
- I choose to think thoughts that bring me closer to my dreams.
- I am in control of my thoughts.
- I choose to be aware of my thoughts.
- I choose to see this differently.
- I choose this to be easy.
- I value my future and invest in it.
- I am moving closer to my dreams.
- I am receiving creative solutions.
- Every day I see more opportunities for me to have the life I want.

I believe your body's emotions and feelings are your first line of communication with your spirit and intuition. When doing this, if you begin feeling resistance to something that you want, lean into that resistance, and allow yourself to discover the root of it. Resistance can show up in the form of heaviness in your body or feeling stuck. It may even feel "icky" or cause a sick feeling in your stomach.

When you feel resistance, ask yourself these questions in order:

- Why do I feel resistance?
- What is this showing me about myself?
- What is this teaching me about my old beliefs?
- What is a new belief that feels better?
- What is a new belief that feels even more in alignment than that?
- I am grateful now that _____ (fill in your new belief here)!

None of this magically happens overnight—it takes work, time, and effort. You might feel overwhelmed at this point but think about how much time you invest in other things in your life. Are those things leading you to the future you want for yourself? Set aside some time every week and look at how much you've accomplished. Remember that what works for someone else may not work for you. Reassess and shift your plan as needed. None of this is written in stone. Be open to failure and to trial and error until your mindset has shifted and evolved. It is easy to get derailed but keep your journal close and don't veer off track. Keep your focus and check in with yourself (or someone else) weekly. It will continually be a process of growth. Time will pass, and you'll see the benefits of that 1° Shift showing up in every part of your life!

10 x 10 x 10 EXERCISE

One exercise I do with my coaching clients is the 10 x 10 x 10. This is something that can be done daily or weekly as a practice, or anytime you need a 1° Shift.

1. Write down 10 things for which you are grateful.
2. Then, write down 10 things you appreciate.
3. Write the 10 things you're manifesting and focus on how excited you would feel to have these things in your life.

I like to write each one back to back. For example:

I am so grateful and thankful for my car. I appreciate that it always gets me where I need to go. I am so excited that my new car is even more reliable and fuel-efficient.

I am so grateful and thankful for the education that I have. I appreciate that it helps me to do my job well. I am so excited that this education opens up massive doors for me.

I am so grateful and thankful for the connection that I have with my kids. I appreciate that we can have candid conversations with open honesty. I am so excited for the impact they are making on the world.

When you do this, you are not only activating the "Law of Thinking" and the "Law of Increase," but you are also bringing in the magnetic aspects of the "Law of Attraction." You become an energetic match for the desires in your heart. Whenever you feel down or insecure, take a moment to apply the 10 x 10 x 10 exercise to experience a massive shift in energy. I often do this exercise out loud while driving.

THE PLACEBO EFFECT & THE POWER OF OUR MINDS

Most people underestimate how powerful the mind really is. One of the best examples of this is the placebo effect and how it impacts shifts in our lives.

In his book, *You Are the Placebo* by Joe Dispenza, Joe presents study after study where people have unknowingly improved their condition without medication through a placebo treatment. He shares about when he was in a horrific biking accident that left him with a broken back and shattered vertebrae. He refused surgery, and even when the doctors told him he would never walk again, his reply was, *"We shall see my friend. We shall see."* He moved in with friends and began visualizing himself walking. Eight weeks later, he did. After defying all odds, he started to train people how to heal themselves and test out the placebo effect for themselves. It isn't the placebo pill itself that makes the difference—it is the mindset and belief that empowers it.

Dispenza shares another story in his book of a man who had cancerous tumors throughout his body. He was denied an experimental trial, but the doctor never told him he was not accepted for the experimental treatment. The doctor gave the patient an IV bag marked with a red "X" on it and told the patient that it would shrink the tumor. The man didn't know that the "treatment" was only saline solution. Two weeks after being on this "treatment," the tumors decreased in size, and the man's health improved. He later saw on the news that the trial he thought he was a part of was unsuccessful, and he became increasingly concerned about it. As a result, the tumors responded with growth. The second time around, the doctor did the same trick, and within weeks, the tumors decreased again, only to be followed by another news report creating stress and concern. The patient died shortly after.

The body also has the power to shift your habits and the way you live your life. Anything is possible when we put our mind to it, but it takes practice to believe it to be true.

Rewiring your brain is a conscious choice to look for positive opportunities. It takes time and practice. This is something you can do! It may be hard and awkward at first, but when you stick to it, you will begin to see a real difference in your life.

Remember, you don't have to do this just once. It is why I keep going back to Stephen R. Covey's quote, *"What is one thing you can do every day to make the biggest impact in your life?"*. Continue making the 1° Shift in the direction of your dreams. Whether you are eliminating clutter or bullshit situations, breaking a bad habit, creating a positive mindset, or encouraging yourself through affirmations, you hold the power to slowly and consistently shift your life for the better.

14

SPIRITUAL LAWS

"Whatever you ask for in prayer, believe that you have received it, and it will be yours."
~ Mark 11:24

Universal Spiritual laws impact every aspect of your life. I like to think of them as gravity—they influence you no matter where you are. While there are many spiritual laws we could talk about, we are going to focus on The Law of Thinking and The Law of Increase.

The Law of Thinking tells us what we <u>think</u> about, we will attract.

The Law of Increase tells us what we <u>focus on</u>, we bring more of in our life.

The more you get clear about your vision for the future you want, the more you are able to focus your priorities. It is easy to see more obstacles than opportunities. We suffer from doubt, and as a result, we don't believe in ourselves enough to reach where we want to go. I'm here to tell you that your mindset shifts your future. Mindset is absolutely everything when it comes to creating and having the life you want.

The first way you can begin to recognize what you're thinking is to look at the life you currently have, as discussed in the previous chapter. Is it a positive life or a negative one? Another way to find clarity is to journal. Some of the most influential people in this world have kept journals. Albert Einstein, Thomas Edison, and Lewis and Clark, heck even Jennifer Aniston, Lady Gaga, and Oprah Winfrey attribute much of their success to journaling.

When we take time to journal, we see a reflection of our mindset on the page. Your life is shown through your reflections of your past thoughts, actions, mindset, and experiences. So far in this book, you've written down your thoughts and your habits, but now it is time to reprogram how you approach what you truly want.

How you talk to yourself here, in this moment, determines how you are able to move forward.

- How do you explain and justify bullshit situations in your life?
- How do you talk to yourself about finances?
- Do you take time to reflect on your love life?
- Do you have positive or negative self-talk in your work environment?

Think for a moment how each of these aspects of your life have played out in the past and in the present moment. What story do you tell or share about each of these areas? The more you tell a story of any kind, the more you breathe life into it.

When I ask my coaching clients to start journaling on a regular basis, they suddenly realize that there is a parallel between what they have been thinking and telling themselves, and how their life presents. Your thoughts have tremendous influence on your life. When you recognize how negative thoughts can influence your life, it's easier to see how the opposite could be true too. When you think positively, you are more likely to experience positive outcomes. While we all hope to think positively every day, some days can be harder than others. The 10 x 10 x 10 practice can help on the more difficult days, and the best part is, it can be done anywhere, anytime.

Talking to yourself positively and using power phrases to consciously move throughout your day affects everything else around you. I've had countless clients try this out, and after just a few weeks, bam! Positive changes start to really happen! With time spent in reflection, you can shift your inner thoughts and the stories you tell yourself to see how it creates a positive impact in your life. This is The Law of Increase in action.

The Law of Increase shows that what you focus on, grows. At this point, you may be coming up with a list of excuses for why you think negative thoughts during your day. The traffic was bad on the way to work. You spilled coffee all over your desk. Your kids are upset from something that happened at school. You don't feel confident in your body, and your outfit just isn't right. You got triggered today while at the store. All of these factors can add to how you talk to yourself and what you think. When you focus on the misery and unhappiness that swirls in your life, the more you create it. When you shift your mindset to a better feeling thought, your energy also shifts from lack to abundance.

In Raymond Holliwell's book *Working with the Law*, he states, "*All action is the result of a thought. It determines the conditions of life, and to have better conditions in life we must first make efforts to organize our thoughts.*"

- When you think about lack, you get more of it.
- When you think about abundance, you get more of it.
- When you think about disease, you get more of it.
- When you think about health, you get more of it.
- When you think about debt, you get more of it.
- Whatever we think in our minds expands out to our life.

For example, you might have your eye on a shiny new car every time you drive past the dealership. You're ready for something new, but it feels unattainable. Once those thoughts creep up, shift your focus to appreciating what you have now and are excited about a new car coming into your life. Let yourself feel the excitement of new possibilities and embody the opportunities that come with it. When you focus this way, your opportunities will increase with your mindset.

Finances are a stressor for most people. It is important to shift your mindset to focus on what you do have. It may sound crazy, but I have flipped the script in my approach to money. Before, I felt drained about bills and stressed about upcoming payments. Now, I see money as a form of energy exchange (value for value). I'm grateful for the service I receive from others, such as heating, electricity, doctor visits, and anything else I take for granted in my daily life. Without these things, life would be quite challenging! Instead of feeling stressed about it, I write down "Thank you for your service," and send it along with the payment. I know what you may be thinking, *"Right Flora, this is all fine and dandy until you don't have any money!"*

I read a story about a Canadian blogger named Kyle MacDonald, who wanted to see the power of "energy exchange" (aka money). He began with a red paperclip and traded it for a different item. He then traded that item for something bigger or better, and so on until the end of the year when he ended up with a house. It's so crazy that it's inspiring!

A few years ago, a friend of mine and I decided to give this challenge a try. Our paperclip was purple, and our first trade was for a marker. Then that was traded for a banana, then a lamp, planter, brass table, and finally, a large lathe saw that we sold for $150. It took us a little under two hours to turn a paperclip into cash money!

Where many people see a lack for something they don't have yet, they are really just not seeing the opportunities that exist. No matter how dire your situation may seem, when you do your best to appreciate what you have *and* think toward abundance in the future, you activate "The Law of Increase" in your life.

Ask yourself:

- What do I have right now?
- How am I already abundant?
- How am I supported by life?
- What would be a fun way to bring in extra money?
- Can I declutter and sell things I no longer use?
- What opportunities exist in my situation?

Keep writing in your journal and don't forget to list all the ways you can shift out of lack and into increase. As you go about your day, give yourself permission to find those opportunities! Whenever I feel overwhelmed, down, or just plain stuck, this is exactly what I do—I look for hidden opportunities. Every shit storm has a silver lining! Sometimes I have to shake my body, or even yell, to release the negative energy caused by life events. When I feel pessimism creeping up, I try to laugh and not let any negativity throw me off my intended path. More often than not, a 1° Shift in mindset is all you need for new opportunities to find their way to you.

SHIFTING THROUGH INTUITION

Prayer is when we talk to God and share our deepest desires. Meditation is when we hear the answers back and feel the peace of what is to come. Intuition is the tiny whispers of how to carry out the answer we've been given.

If you're having trouble changing your thoughts, create space in your day to get into a creative, intentional state. When do you do your best thinking? Is it first thing in the morning? At night right before you go to sleep? Is it while you're in the shower, or outside hiking in the wilderness? Pick a time and place that inspires your best thoughts and set your intention to find your clarity of thought—what you desire most.

Ask yourself what you really want and then listen for that answer. Pray to learn what is best for you in this moment and pay close attention to what bubbles up from your energy source. Visualize your desire and think about how it would feel to receive it in full. As you meditate, don't allow doubts to creep in and when they do—because they will—practice shifting your attention toward your desire straight away.

Let your intuition be your guide. When you tap into your intuition, allow your body to give you signals. I believe we are spirits embodied, and the first piece of information we get from the Universe is through our physical body. Pay attention to the "Clairs":

- Clair-Sentient—Clear Feeling
- Clair-Cognoscente—Clear Knowing

- Clair-Voyant—Clear Seeing
- Clair-Audence—Clear Hearing
- Clair-Fragrant—Clear Smelling
- Clair-Gustance—Clear Tasting

Tuning into your intuition is just like tuning into a radio frequency and paying attention to the energy that you perceive. Everything is born out of connection. Connect to Source and sit quietly. Notice what you pick up. Pay attention to what you feel, think, hear, and experience. The more you relax and focus on this, the more you will receive and understand. When you receive an answer, respond to the clarity with gratitude.

The most powerful prayer you can say to yourself and the Universe is *"Thank you."* When good things happen in our lives, we automatically lean toward thankfulness. When we pause to say thank you, it pulls us deeper into a state of appreciation for life. It all goes back to what we focus on. Gratitude is directly correlated with receiving. Everything that happens for us—good or bad—is an opportunity for us to move into a new state of being. If we experience something that is negative, it is easy to let it suck us further away from how we want to be. Remember, everything is happening FOR you, not TO you.

If you can find the positives in situations that are hard, difficult, or just plain shitty, it can fuel appreciation to be all the more powerful. Whenever life throws you unexpected curveballs, you can still say "thank you" with the understanding that there is growth opportunity within every trial.

When my two boys were in Marine Corps boot camp, it felt like they were gone forever. Being a Marine myself, I knew how difficult Marine boot camp would be, but I trusted that they were following their dreams. The two times we were able to talk over the phone while they were away, our time was limited, but no matter how brief, I treasured our calls together. I cried with joy because I held so much appreciation for my boys. Just hearing their voices would make me say a prayer of gratitude.

It is easy to be thankful during short periods of joy like speaking to your kid who is far away living their dream but trying to be appreciative when things are messy or hard isn't quite as easy. Challenge yourself to shift your mindset when times are hard. There is wisdom in the moment when you pause to say, "thank you." See how it can shift your mood.

Remember, the Law of Increase here. When you focus on gratitude, it will come in abundance. When you shift to focus on the positive, those negative feelings no longer hold power over you. The situation will decrease in intensity, and you'll be able to see opportunities you can take to improve your life. If there is anything that can make the most impact on your life, it is saying "thank you" for every little thing. Practice the 10 x 10 x 10 daily or anytime you want to shift your energy immediately.

ENVIRONMENT

Our environments have a massive impact on our focus, mindset, positivity, health, and overall wellbeing. Everything you see has meaning, and most of the things you see and recognize are things connected to your past. When it comes to the environment you live in, how do you feel when you look at your living room, bedroom, or kitchen? Do you feel inspired? Drained? What about when you look at your wardrobe? How you feel when you look at things in your life are clues to what feels supportive and what doesn't.

Over time, we create associations with objects we own, like the negative energy from paying the bills with the checkbook or excitement when seeing the coffee maker. Rather than continuing in that sinking feeling, shift your outlook by changing how things look. Perhaps you could purchase a new checkbook cover or pay your bills in a different room than you usually do. This brings forth a new feeling and outlook every time you go to pay the bills. This physical reminder will help you look for positive association.

The same can happen when you feel like you've let yourself down in looking after your wellbeing. You may look in the mirror and feel flabby, which is a reactionary thought pattern. You may have been thinking about this for a while, and now, it is just a habit to associate negative feelings every time you see yourself in a mirror. Instead, change the script!

Look at yourself and say your 10 x 10 x 10 out loud:

- I am grateful for my body. I love and appreciate how much my body has carried me through these years.
- I am grateful that my body has birthed two babies, undergone several surgeries, and is still strong and healthy.
- I love and appreciate how supported I feel in my body.
- I am grateful that my body lets me know what feels good and what doesn't feel good by the emotions and feelings I experience throughout the day.
- I'm so excited that my body is getting healthier and stronger each day.

Place sticky notes on your mirror with power phrases on them to shift your script and allow yourself to feel and appreciate that shift in self-talk. When you choose to change how you respond to a trigger, that trigger loses power over you.

Just as your mirror acts as a visual cue for habitual thoughts, the places we go can also trigger a shift in the way we feel. What places do you frequent when you're feeling "off"? I often wander to Whole Foods, West Elm, a local bookstore, Caribou Coffee (a local coffee franchise), or Target. When I walk into these places, I can feel my energy shift. I feel lighter and more fluid.

Years ago, after a messy divorce, I found myself getting lost in these stores and had to ask myself, *"How can I recreate this feeling in my life and in my own home?"* I decided to do a little research as it pertained to places where my energy positively shifted.

I asked myself the following questions:

- What colors are in these places?
- What music is playing?
- What kind of lighting do they have?
- Why does being here make me feel so good?
- What elements are here that feel good to me (textures, patterns, etc.)?

I noticed a trend and started to mindfully bring those elements that spoke to me from each space into my home. I decluttered my house and only kept what I loved in each room. I mind-fully thought about colors and their impact on my mood. I chose the colors for each room, recognizing my intentions. I systematically and intentionally brought changes into my home and life that felt good and filled me with peace and joy. If it felt cluttered or off in any way, it didn't stay! Now, people always mention that my house feels so calm and relaxing to be in—that it's like a mini vacation spot they could just get lost in. That is exactly the energy I was aiming to bring in.

By consciously creating my surroundings, I was able to pay attention to my energy in other parts of my life and become aware of what I needed to address when situations didn't feel good. My home used to be so packed with clutter that it triggered sensory overload. In that kind of space, it is hard to relax and unplug enough to hear what your intuition is trying to tell you. By intentionally creating your living space you open the door to take even better care of yourself.

SELF-CARE

Let's look at self-care. Your thoughts are linked to the actions you take daily. Those actions determine how you feel physically, mentally, and emotionally.

When we feel "off" or "funky", it's hard to know how to get out of the funk, especially if we don't know what makes us feel our best. One way to understand how to get out of a funk is to look at what helps you feel your best. I do this by creating a "Best Self List." It's where you write down everything you do that results in you feeling your best. This has shifted slightly over the years, but for the most part, it holds true year-round. I keep this list taped up in my home, and when I'm feeling off, I ask myself, *"What am I not doing?"*

When writing down your "Best Self List", think about all aspects of your life and what you're doing. Writing out this list has helped so many of my clients because it serves as a reminder to find things that help them when life feels off. When we feel "off" or out of sorts, we can pause and ask ourselves, *"What am I not doing and what could I be doing to feel better?"* Then, turn to your list and find something that will shift you back to feeling centered.

This list serves as a way to prepare you for an overall better outlook on life. The more you give time to the things that fill you up, the more equipped you are to handle bullshit situations that happen in life. For me, I love to declutter (and yes, I actually enjoy it!), but to others, that may feel like a chore. We're all different and have different ways of approaching self-care.

To help you start your list, here are a few acts of self-care that might work for you:

Sing	Dance
Paint	Pray
Meditate	Take a walk or hike
Read	Call a friend
Cook	Bake
Take a bubble bath	Color
Sightsee	Take a nap
Go for a drive	Garden
Exercise	Get a manicure
Play video games	Write someone a letter
Have sex with a partner or ourselves	Send a care package
Go to a movie	Fish
Send someone flowers	Journal
Declutter	Rearrange a room
Plan a picnic	Play with your cat or dog
Visit a body of water (lake, ocean, sea, river)	Perform a random act of kindness

One of my students was having trouble with her meditation practice, so I recommended that she try coloring. She bought a swear-word coloring book for adults. She told me, *"Nothing says 'calm' like coloring the phrase 'dickhead' in calm blue tones while listening to angst-ridden music."* I laughed so hard, but she's right, that worked for her!

This is one example of how a "Best Self List" can look:

- Get 8 hours of sleep a night—to feel rested and think clearly.
- Drink 3 liters of water a day—to feel hydrated and aid digestion.
- Take daily supplements—to care for mental and long-term health.
- Workout for 30 minutes a day—to feel strong and centered.
- Meditate for 5 minutes every afternoon—to feel less chaos in the day.
- Go hiking with my dog—to seek clarity and connect with my dog and nature.
- Call my kids every other day—to nurture our bond and connection.
- Make love to my partner daily—to deepen our connection and bond.
- Declutter my house once a week—to keep the clutter at bay and not feel anxious.
- Do an Inbox Zero each week—to reduce overwhelm.
- Be outside in the sun for at least 20 min a day—to regulate mood.
- Watch/read something by my favorite comedian daily —to laugh and get out of my head.

This list is just the tip of the iceberg. There are so many ways you can fill yourself to feel really good every day. Break out that notebook and make a list of your own. This list can serve as a reference or a daily ritual to help you feel supported. Time for self-care will give you more energy and focus throughout your day to do the things (and feel the things) that you want to experience. All of these steps are a ripple effect that start inside and move exponentially outward into every part of your life.

PART V
YOUR TIME IS NOW

15

THE PERFECT TIME

"By thought, the thing you want is brought to you; by action you receive it."
~ Wallace D. Wattles

We often hold the excuse that we aren't ready to take action because the timing doesn't feel right. We tell ourselves that the circumstances aren't right, so we can't put a plan into motion. "Only when _____ happens, can I do _____."

If not now, when?

How many things do you let slip before taking the time for inspired action? What will it take for you to take steps toward a positive solution?

Many of us feel suffocated, lonely, restricted, and abused. Clients come to me for sessions and break down in tears because they have been waiting and waiting for the right time to take action. It breaks my heart to see what people put up with in their lives. When is the perfect time to make a change? When is it time to break the cycle?

There is no perfect time. That ideal timing to make the right move in your life will never, ever come.

I'll let you in on a secret though: That time you have been waiting for is this moment. Right now.

Whenever you put up with a situation because it doesn't feel like the right time to change it, you are wasting precious time. I know it is scary as hell to address these issues, but that is why the 1° Shift Method can help you right at this moment. The best method to affect change is just 1° at a time in so many circumstances.

Life can be so much more when you no longer let yourself suffer through difficult situations. That type of self-sacrifice and martyrdom serves no one (not even you). Look at what you have been sweeping under the rug over the years. It is time to lift it up and deal with it.

Most people don't see the need to change until they reach a breaking point. They wait until they get fired from the job they hated, land in the hospital from a health issue, or are abandoned by their partner. I promise you that you don't have to wait until you hit rock bottom. You can decide today that you want something different for your life. You have the power to act on that decision. Simply commit to shifting 1° at a time.

Mary called me struggling with an addiction problem and feeling trapped in an abusive relationship. She was scared to move forward. Her fear held her in place, but over six months, she finally made enough shifts in her life to get clean and leave her relationship.

Kathleen was binge-eating sweets, avoiding working out, and going down a negative spiral of depression. After only one month of working with her, her blood sugar was regulated, and she had lost five pounds.

Michelle was in a job that she hated and felt suffocated by her marriage. After three months, she had changed jobs and revived her marriage. She and her husband took a second honeymoon and renewed their vows.

You don't have to reach a breaking point to create a shift in your life. Your time is now.

COMING INTO MY OWN—CLARITY

On the eve of my dad's death, my entire immediate family was gathered in my dad's living room around his bed. We started sharing what we love and appreciate about each other. One of my step-sisters looked at me and said, "I love and appreciate how you reinvent yourself every couple of years."

The comment took me by surprise. I knew that I was constantly trying new ways to live my life to the fullest, but I never considered viewing it as re-inventing myself. I knew when things felt off or were not working anymore, I would do a 1° Shift and change my course without waiting for the circumstances to be perfect. I wasn't always this way, though. It was a lesson that took me a long time to learn, and life didn't spare me for the easy version. The more I tuned into what was working and what wasn't, the more I was able to gain clarity on what to shift next in my life.

When I filed for my third divorce, I was scared. My ex made over six figures a year, and I was fearful of not making it on my own financially. In turn, I stayed with him longer than I should have. Little did I know that within 18 months of leaving him, my income surpassed his by nearly double. He had convinced me that I would never be able to make it without him. When shit hit the fan, and I hit rock bottom, I put on my big girl pants and told myself, *"I can do this. I've done this before. I have survived on my own a long time before I met him."* With gritted teeth and sweaty palms, I harnessed my courage and asked for a divorce. I was terrified, but I gave myself over to the Universe and said, *"Y'all gotta make this happen because I don't know what to do next."*

I survived! I made it work on my own just fine. I allowed myself clarity of thought–I got crystal clear about the kind of life I wanted. I asked for help from those around me and humbled myself enough to receive it. I did so well on my own that I felt foolish for convincing myself to stay with him for as long as I did. None of the things I worried about was a problem in my new chapter of life. I'm not saying it was easy, because major life changes never are, but it was not even close to being as difficult as I had made it out to be. I survived the change I needed, and you can, too.

FEAR OF FAILURE—COURAGE

A big reason why people put off making life decisions is the fear surrounding them: fear of failure, fear of the unknown, fear of what could go wrong. This is absolutely a genuine emotion and should be taken seriously. You never want to take a big decision lightly, but learning where that fear is coming from is important.

Thomas Edison tried 10,000 times to create the light bulb before he actually got it to work! A reporter once asked him how it felt to fail 10,000 times, and he said that he didn't fail 10,000 times—it just took him that many tries to make it work.

How many mistakes have you made? How many failures have you experienced in life? Most of us cannot even count the number of times we've fallen.

I remember standing in the kitchen one day with my oldest son. He had recently turned 18 and was giving me a strange look. I asked him, *"What's up? What's with the look?"*

"Adults don't know what they're doing, do they?" He asked curiously.

"Nope! We just wing it and hope for the best! Sometimes we have some experience to know what to do, but if we've never done something before, we either wing it, Google it, or ask someone for help."

He was blown away and bemused at my response. How would your life look if you knew that everyone else was out there just winging it too?

I like to think of mistakes or failures as discoveries—a discovery of what works, what doesn't, and what is ultimately valuable for my life. I have learned that when I marry a codependent person that the relationship is going to be messy. I also know if I eat a pint of ice cream, I'm going to be bloated because I'm lactose intolerant.

The failures and mistakes we experience in life become discoveries because they teach us lessons about ourselves. When situations don't turn out how you thought they would, try not to place judgment on yourself or engage in negative self-talk. You are doing the best you can! Shift your inner dialogue to, *"Okay, well, that didn't work out the way I planned. Let's try something else."* This is where the power of mentorship comes in. Who in your life has been through the trials of which you are afraid? Ask for their guidance or hire a coach to help you through the parts of your life that you don't know how to deal with.

Think about what you want to change in your life. What is the biggest fear that is holding you in place from reaching that change? What is the worst possible scenario to happen if that fear became true? Now, think about the best scenario that

147

could happen. This helps you not only gain clarity of thought, but it also looks at the source of your fear. Harness your courage and use it to step into action toward your vision. While doing this, it's important to keep your vision intact. Place your pursuit in a positive light and utilize your mind's eye to see your endeavor through to your ultimate success.

I once had a client share with me that she was having an issue at work and was desperate to bring it up to the administration, but fear kept her from doing anything. I walked her through the exercise to uncover what would be the worst thing that could happen, which would be her getting fired. She was terrified, but she also was burnt out and open to having time off. The best thing that could happen would be for the administration to take matters seriously and resolve the issue for the staff. Once we walked through the possible steps and outcomes that could happen, she realized she wasn't happy with her job at all. Getting fired suddenly felt like the better of the two options! When she had her "aha" moment, she made an exit plan. She now owns a highly successful spa and salt cave, and more importantly, she is much happier!

When we think about failure, our fears have been ingrained in our neural pathways to avoid pain and disappointment. If you take the time to look at the best and worst case scenario, you'll soon see that there are many ways situations can play out. Taking a look at the best and worst cases allows you to take the emotional charge out of it and prepare for what is to come in the future.

When you are able to rewrite the script of your life, you can begin to look at failures as discoveries. Taking that 1° Shift towards the life that you want, rather than succumbing to the fear of everything that *could* happen, is where the magic happens.

BUILDING MOMENTUM—CONFIDENCE

When trying to make life shifts, we might Google everything we can, listen to podcasts, take courses online, or sit with a mountain of books, but none of that actually gets us to where we want to be.

It isn't until we put what we know and feel into action that we finally get somewhere.

Reading and learning will help you to find both clarity and courage when it comes to the next steps you want to take. When your discoveries become inspired action, you then empower yourself to keep going. When you keep making little shifts, you build the momentum necessary to reach your intention.

I started a home organizing business in 1997 as a side gig. I hosted in-person consultations and group classes, but it wasn't until 2009 that I decided to get serious about it. I finally asked myself, *"What if I worked on this more than part-time?"* I had been putting it off with many excuses, but I finally realized that if I waited until my kids were older, I would never follow through with this dream. So, I did it. After I made my first instructional video on YouTube, I knew I needed to stop overthinking it and just show up to share my gifts to the world.

I taught what I knew. It wasn't *"the end all, be all, and I know it all."* I simply shared what I knew. It was fun, easy, and I loved being on video! It felt natural to me.

When I was younger, I always felt like other people *knew* something I didn't. It took me a long time to realize that everybody is just winging it, and we are all in this together. We are all going through the same thing. We have different perspectives and problems, but it all boils down to the same thing. No one is better than anyone else. Some people may be more experienced, yet while one person may be strong in one area, they also have weaknesses in another. We make up for one another's weaknesses and strengths. It is the way we complement one another in growth.

Everyone's an expert at something. We all have something we enjoy doing and are good at. For instance, I watched my sister make over a hundred jars of jam in two weeks. She's good at it and could easily teach a class about making jam. The key to all of this is to see how amazingly gifted you are. Be willing to recognize the gifts you already have and start acting on them! Don't wait. Give yourself permission to feel the fear of it all—and go for it anyway!

DON'T WAIT FOR MOTIVATION

In *The 5 Second Rule*, Mel Robbins discusses how motivation is fleeting because it derives from an unreliable emotion that is layered among factors that change every day. Our emotions ebb and flow, depending on how our day is going. Whether you've been fired from a job, lost a loved one unexpectedly, received bad news, argued with a friend, or are not sleeping well—it all contributes to motivation, for better or for worse.

You've probably been in a situation where you've convinced yourself to wait to do something about a problem. So, you wait and wait, just holding out for the motivation to deal with it. Soon enough, you're stuck.

Instead of feeling stuck, I look at motivation as a brief glimpse into the future. We get excited at the prospect of having this new thing in our life, and we entertain how different our life could be accordingly. Then, life kicks back in. We get busy and come up with every excuse in the book that prevents us from doing what we want or need to do.

We have to focus on the small changes and shifts we can make every day to reach the life we want. When you don't feel motivated to take action or make change, those little 1° Shifts help you stick with your intentions. Don't get me wrong, there will be times that this feels like the most challenging action to take. You might be feeling fear around committing to change, and I know just how easy it can be to fall back into old patterns. After all, we are creatures of habit! If you recognize just one change that you can commit to, then it becomes easier to stay on track and set other little shifts in motion. Committing to the 1° Shift Method is what can drive your mindset toward improving positive habits.

You don't have to wait for motivation to act. I know change can be scary, but life will not fix itself. You hold the key to saving yourself from stressful situations, negative environments, and bad habits. Only you have the power to create lasting change in your life, but the longer you put it off, the more challenging it will be to accomplish the task or address and overcome the problem you're dealing with.

TAKING THE FIRST STEP

You may be desperate to change your life for the better, but something still holds you back from taking that first step. Why is it so hard to make that 1° Shift happen in your life?

We've all bought into the lie that we have to feel ready for change. We assume that someday we will have every ounce of courage and confidence to make the life we want happen. Somehow, that day never seems to come. Our brains caution us against anything that feels uncomfortable, difficult, or scary. It creates hesitation around perceived risk, much like the fears we tell ourselves that we discussed earlier. It is a survival mechanism built on our experiences throughout life. Yet,

151

change requires us to take a first step of courage, beyond what feels difficult or frightening.

When I make videos, I often try to clean up the house before I click "record." I cannot tell you how many times I've delayed filming because my house was a mess! Do you know what else is messy? Life. Yet, we wait for everything to be perfect before we take any steps toward action. Allow yourself to engage the courage within! When you make excuses and procrastinate, you're only hurting yourself. This was personally very hard for me because I am a perfectionist, but I've come to accept that my best is going to change from day to day, and that's okay.

Some days I'll have super-charged energy, while other days I feel lazy and unmotivated. If something does need to happen on a certain day, or I catch myself putting it off, I know that I have to show up as the best version I can that day. All we can do is try our best.

Don Miguel Ruiz has a fabulous book called *The Four Agreements.* In the book, he discusses how *our best* changes from day to day. We have to give ourselves grace to show up without judgement and do the best we can every day. Like we've talked about before in this book, energy ebbs and flows just like the seasons in nature. Allow yourself to feel how you feel but be willing to take small shifts toward what you truly want.

Time is the only thing we can't take back. Life will not wait around for you. If you allow yourself to receive and experience love, hardship, heartache, joy, and everything in between, you open up doors to living and thriving in a life by design. You already have the courage and self-confidence inside of you to deal with what life has thrown at you. You don't have to feel like you are in survival mode or waiting until shit really hits the fan to do something about your life. Mel Robbins says, "Your life comes down to your decisions, and when you change your decisions, you will change everything." You may be one decision away from changing your marriage, improving the environment at work, or completely shifting your life for the better.

Take a moment to reflect on what conditions you are waiting for before you make change happen in your life. Instead of dwelling on when you can start, think about one thing you can do right now. What could move you in the direction you want to go? What shift can catapult you toward how you want to feel? The perfect conditions for change simply won't come, that perfect time is now. Right here. Take that one step towards your 1° Shift today.

16

PUTTING IT ALL TOGETHER

"The journey of a thousand miles begins with one step."
~ Lao Tzu

U p until this point, I've presented the 1° Shift in various ways, but there is a method that can be applied step by step. This is where everything comes together.

Here is the exact 1° Shift Method:

- Step #1—What is the situation? (Fact + Feeling)
- Step #2—What do I want instead?
- Step #3—Am I willing to do something about the issue?
- Step #4—What is the opportunity hidden inside the obstacle?
- Step #5—What is one small step I can take right now? (Your 1° Shift)
- Step #6—Commit to taking action.
- Step #7—Look for the evidence of it working. (The result)

Step #1. What is the situation? Fact + Feeling

Where are you at in life right now? Where in your life are you looking for change?

What is going on in that part of your life? Don't think about what *might* be going on—think about *what is actually happening*.

Take a look at your feelings around this situation. Notice how it feels in your mind and in your body. What emotions are present?

This can get raw, and honestly, pretty gritty. The first time I worked through these steps in my life was in 2003. I left South Africa with my two sons and moved in with my middle sister. Getting on the plane to Saint Paul, Minnesota, was an important step forward, but I could not stop there. If my life was really going to change, I had to be honest with myself.

This first step is not easy by any means. I spent my first few months in this newfound life in Minnesota, wallowing in self-pity. I had an affair, quit my job, and ran away from everything in my life. I had to come to terms with everything I'd done before I could begin to make positive change in my life. It was difficult and painful, but it's what I had to do.

It is important to know where you are at. This is a step many people try to avoid. They stumble right out of the gate and refuse to be honest with themselves. It isn't always intentional, but there is a fine line between what is actually going on, and what you "think" is going on.

If you've been doing the exercises throughout this book, you are already ahead of the game. Go back to your list of bullshit from Chapter 4. Take a look at the things causing you pain, hardship, and fear from your brain dump. That's this step! If you've already written it down, you're ready for Step #2.

Step #2. What do I want instead?

Do you remember the scene in *Alice in Wonderland* when Alice is lost in the woods? She encountered the Cheshire Cat and asked, *"Would you tell me, please, which way I ought to go from here?"*

The Cat replied, *"That depends a good deal on where you want to go."*

"I don't much care where," Alice said.

"Then it doesn't matter which way you go."

There is wisdom in the Cheshire Cat's words that it doesn't really matter *where* you go until you know where you *want* to go. You can stay still, run backwards or step forward. It's your choice.

When we moved to Minnesota, my boys and I would retreat to the library together and get lost in the pages of another world. One day, while sitting on the library floor surrounded by books, I saw a glimpse of a book titled, *Write it Down, Make it Happen: Knowing what You Want and Getting It!* by Henriette Anne Klauser. The book talked about how to figure out what you wanted and how to get it. *"Great,"* I thought, *"I have no idea what I want. I just know I don't want what life is throwing at me now."* I devoured the book and became clear about what I truly wanted.

Pause for a moment and imagine the burdens that you've experienced being lifted. How would that feel? What is preventing you from reaching that feeling? Be honest here but also leave space to be realistic. Remember the giant house I really wanted? I had to come to terms with the fact I did not want to clean such a big house. I actually wanted something more modest, something simpler. What's important in this step is that what you want, need, or desire doesn't have to appeal to anyone else. This is a space dedicated to what is important to you and what direction you want to turn your life toward.

Step #3. Am I willing to do something about the issue?

When I was sitting on the beach in South Africa all those years ago wallowing in my problems, I knew something needed to change. In a single moment of clarity, I gathered the willpower to get my life back. I was 100% willing to do whatever it took to shift. It may seem simple at first to take that first step, but often, we aren't willing to do anything about the problems we are experiencing.

A client I was working with had those same feelings. She struggled with a challenging marriage as her spouse repeatedly cheated on her. She knew she wanted a divorce but felt there were too many obstacles standing in her way—a new job, a new baby coming (in addition to two other children), and a new house. She was not willing to make a change at that point in her life.

Step #4. What is the opportunity hidden inside the obstacle?

We have all felt like there are problems in our way, but what if we looked for opportunities within the problem instead?

In the past, my main obstacle was myself. After leaving South Africa, I felt like I was in a race to leave my sister's house to find a job and provide for my family, but there was no way I could find a job that paid for daycare, food, rent, and everything else life threw at me. It took me a while to realize that my sister had provided the opportunity for me to rest, recharge, and regroup. Some days, that meant being able to sleep and reset my mind, body, and spirit. If I didn't have the opportunity to rest, I could have easily fallen back into the same bad trap of habits all over again. While not having a job at the time felt like a huge obstacle, it actually led me to my ultimate goal and the opportunity to regroup, get honest, and make a plan.

Shift your focus away from the obstacle itself and look a little deeper. What opportunities can you see in the problems in front of you? Every obstacle we face in life has opportunities hidden inside of it if we are willing to look for them. It may even lead you to unexpected opportunities and shift you just a little closer to where you want to be in life.

Step #5. What is one small step I can take right now?

This whole book is about making one small shift at a time. It might be as simple as waking up a little earlier or looking for new job opportunities in the evenings. Those simple steps toward the life you want is all it takes to make long-term change. You just have to take that step forward.

What can often help us get on track is someone else holding us accountable. My sister was always there for me, but she wasn't going to sit idly while I fell into the same old bad habits. She held me accountable and wouldn't let me delay my progress toward change any longer by letting me wallow in feeling sorry for myself. She knew I needed the time to recalibrate and gave me the space to do so, but she encouraged me to focus on the aspects of my life that needed to get back on track. I started with little steps. I looked for the right job, searched for a used car, and cleaned up after my family to keep clutter at bay. Every day, every one of those little steps helped me walk closer to achieving greater clarity for my life.

Step #6. Commit to taking action

In Minnesota, I felt discouraged when looking for opportunities. Nothing seemed to be the right fit. I knew I didn't want to sit behind a desk all day and needed more of a people-focused job. After a long search, I wound up turning toward the

Veterans Affairs Department for help with job placement. While discussing options, I learned that the injuries that I sustained during a skydiving accident while in the Marines gave me the qualification requirement for a V.A. Vocational Rehabilitation scholarship. I applied through an extensive application and interview process and received a full scholarship to college. I was able to earn a Bachelor of Science in General Business with a double minor in Marketing and Management. None of that could have even begun to spin into motion without those daily shifts I was taking toward my dream life.

When you make little shifts happen every day, a world of possibilities opens that you never considered to be an option before. We can't predict what lies around the corner in life, but we may find ourselves walking down unexpected paths toward our dreams. We just have to be willing to take the action of walking forward.

Step #7. Look for the evidence of it working—the result

Consider what it looks like to pop one kernel of popcorn every day. You won't see the evidence of progress at first, but over time, you'll have a full bowl of popcorn! The same goes for that 1° Shift in your life. After a while, results will begin to reveal themselves.

Each little shift helps you break out of old habits and form new, healthier ones that put you on the path toward changing your life. The process will gradually become easier and more natural as you progress. It's happened to me, my kids, and every client with whom I work. Change is possible.

EVERYDAY ISSUES

One of the biggest questions people ask about the 1° Shift Method is if it can also be applied to small things, not just the big things. Absolutely yes! In fact, I encourage you to apply the 1° Shift Method to smaller things first. This helps lay down the foundation for it to become second nature to you. I apply this method to everything in my life that feels "off".

Let's walk through this together. Take, for example, that one day you wake up feeling "off" and a bit funky. To get back on track, apply these steps:

Step #1—What is the situation? Fact + Feeling

I feel funky. I got enough sleep but am feeling restless.

Step #2—What do I want instead?

I want to feel energized and have fun with the day.

Step #3—Am I willing to do something about the issue?

Yes!

Step #4—What is the opportunity hidden inside the obstacle?

I feel that the obstacle is if I stay home, then I will continue to feel off throughout the day. The opportunity is for me to go to the park and play with my dog.

Step #5—What is one small step I can take right now? (Your 1° pivot)

Put on my shoes and go for a walk.

Step #6—Commit to taking action

I will go for a walk.

Step #7—Look for the evidence of it working—the result

I'm done with my walk and feel energized and had fun playing with my dog!

Utilizing these steps can help you shift out of a bad mood, a stressful conversation with a friend or spouse, or to remove yourself from anything that feels out of alignment with your higher self.

The whole purpose of the 1° Shift Method is to change your life with grace and ease toward where you want to be. It will help you see aspects of your life that no longer resonate with you and allow you to slowly shift to healthier habits, boundaries, relationships, and to feel empowered to have the life you want.

WHAT IF I DON'T SEE RESULTS?

I get this question all the time.

What if you have put every step into place and feel excited about progress but then are left thinking, *"What the hell, I don't see any results at all!"* When you apply the 1° Shift Method, you are heading down a brand-new path. You've never seen this path before, but being a creature of habit, you may want to turn back toward what is comfortable and familiar.

Your brain is wired to look for the familiar, and it is likely that you aren't feeling (or seeing) results because you aren't looking for the evidence of new things that come as a result of your 1° Shifts.

You may be walking toward a new goal but feel distracted, and you continue to look back with your mind and heart directed toward where you have been. It's natural to want to focus on your past viewpoint. You aren't alone in this. It is what we are wired to do! As creatures of habit, we look for the constants in our lives, but that is where we can get pulled into old familiar habits that hold us back.

Recognize that what you had is no longer what you want. Just as if you were walking East, and then suddenly you shift your body by 1° while still looking East, you're not going to see the results you had anticipated. When you focus on where you have been over and over again to see the problems, conflict, and unhappiness that old path brought into your life, you may find yourself stuck there. It will only lead to more conflict and more unhappiness if you dwell in what you had before. You have to be willing to look at a new path toward who you want to become. Continue to hone that vision and tie your intention and behavior to it regularly.

When you make a 1° Shift in your life, look for evidence that the shift is working. Change always creates a result, just as every action has a reaction. Looking for what's new will help you stay motivated and allow you to continue making additional shifts. The next time you don't see any change happening, ask yourself, "What is different today?" Speak it out loud if you have to. This is all part of ownership, and it's what allows you to continue building confidence in your vision.

You must be intentional about seeing the results of your newfound behavior. The little things that are changing are everywhere around you. You just need to hone your eyes to see them and claim them for the life you are in the process of creating. This is clarity, courage, and confidence at work—and this is how dreams find their way into reality.

AFTERWORD

At the time of writing this, I am here in Wisconsin during the transition from Winter to Spring. There is still some ice around, but it is beginning to melt. Some days are sunny, some are not, but we're starting to see the weather shift. The other day, my partner and I were out driving and pulled over when we spotted an ice dam. We walked over to it, mesmerized by the sight. The river was dammed with so much melting ice that it had forged an entirely new path for the water to run down. Ice was piled like logs along the side of the river, and we spotted about 50 robins perched upon it. It was the first time we'd seen robins all season. To think, we would have never seen it or even known those birds were perched there if we didn't break the routine to stop and get out of the car.

These signs and changes are happening all around us in nature. It's the same with your life! Take the time to stop and reflect. What do you see? The decision to pause and reflect is one action that can catalyze massive success in your life—a game-changer that helps you build momentum. When you make your 1° Shifts, you will begin to see the differences show up in your life, and you see these differences through reflection. Soon, the lifestyle becomes routine. It's truly addictive, and you'll want to continue shifting your life. You'll want to empower yourself again and again. Every little and big shift will bring with it the confidence to keep going. You'll feel yourself gravitating toward the life you've always dreamed of —a life that is fluid, fun, and easy. A life that you're excited to live.

It's true that we are all different and that each of us have different paths, perspectives, and intentions, but there are some things in life that are universal; there are some things that are as true as nature itself. One of these things is the desire for happiness. If you take no other truth from this book, take this: Your happiness is entirely within your control. If you can envision a successful life, you can design it. If you fall off track, you can make a shift and get back on track. The power to create the life you want lives in you and is fully accessible shift upon shift.

If you stay consistent to your 1° Shifts, your dream life will one day encompass you. There will come a moment when you'll look at your life and wonder, *"Why am I so happy?"* You'll realize it's because you are living your vision. You've eliminated the clutter in your life, you've shifted your mindset, you've cleared all the bullshit, and you've found your pathway of pursuit. You've embraced the simplicity of lasting change.

Give yourself permission to make that first 1° Shift. Your time is now.

MY ROCK BOTTOM/BONUS CHAPTER

Want to learn more about what brought me to a place of
writing this book for you?
Visit https://florasage.com/1degreebook/

.

RESOURCES

RESOURCES MENTIONED BY FLORA SAGE

- Simplify—10 Day Declutter Extravaganza! Program
- 1° Shift Tribe Membership
- Mastermind Mafia Program
- Year in Reverse Book

BOOKS REFERENCED

- *Atomic Habits* by James Clear
- *First Things First* by Stephen R. Covey
- *The Power of Habit* by Charles Duhigg
- *Choice Theory* by William Glasser, M.D.
- *Destructive Emotions, A Scientific Dialogue with the Dalai Lama* narrated by Daniel Goleman
- *Think and Grow Rich* by Napoleon Hill
- *Write It Down, Make It Happen* by Henriette Anne Klauser
- *Wake Up and Live* by Dorothea Brand

- *You Are the Placebo* by Joe Dispenza
- *Working with The Law* by Raymond Holliwell
- *The Four Agreements* by Don Miguel Ruiz
- *The 5-Second Rule* by Mel Robbins

ADDITIONAL RECOMMENDED READS

- *The Strangest Secret* by Earl Nightingale
- *Mini Habits* by Stephen Guise
- *How to be an Adult* by David Richo
- *7 Habits of Highly Effective People* by Stephen R. Covey
- *The 10-Second Philosophy* by Derek Mills
- *The Science of Getting Rich* by Wallace D. Wattles

ADDITIONAL BOOKS BY FLORA

- *The Simple Sabbat*
- *The 29 Day Moon Challenge*
- *The Yay Factor Daily Guide*
- *Flora's Fragrances*
- *Year In Reverse*
- *Year In Reverse Workbook*

APPENDIX

THE BLUEPRINT FOR SIGNIFICANT CHANGE

EXERCISE #1 (FROM CHAPTER 3)

1 - Take out three pieces of paper.

2 - Label the top of the first piece of paper, "List 1"

Write out the top four things you spend the most time on during the day, outside of your main occupation. This could be driving to work, looking at social media, caring for kids / family, social engagements, etc.

3 - Label the top of the second piece of paper, "List 2"

Write out the four things you routinely do each day that are outside of true obligation. Such as, have your morning coffee, exercise, read, listen to podcasts, cook dinner, etc. These are things you generally do not negotiate out of your routine.

4 - Label the top of the last piece of paper, "List 3"

Write out your top four life priorities. These are things you feel you must have to achieve a "successful" life. Examples include financial independence, healthy lifestyle, and being a good parent.

Now, place these three lists side by side and compare.

Do any of the items on the lists match up?

Using the three lists, you can intentionally craft a blueprint for the life that's meaningful for you. The key is to take your top four life priorities (list 3) and marry them into the things that take up the most time during your day (list 1) and those things you MUST do each day (list 2).

The goal is to be very intentional about not just what you're doing in a given day but also why and how. It is this type of focus that will allow you to create the daily life you are excited about.

With that said, begin again:

List 1: Write out the top four things you want to spend the most time doing.

List 2: Write out four things you WILL or MUST do each day.

List 3: Write out your top four priorities.

DIALOGUE SCRIPT

EXERCISE #2 (FROM CHAPTER 5)

Speaking your truth simply means being honest with yourself and the other person about how you feel without blame or implication.

When the time comes, and you've gathered your courage to have the tough conversation about boundaries, it can be helpful to prepare by using this dialogue script:

"When_____ happens, I feel_____ because _____.

What I really need is _____."

The crucial part of this dialogue script is taking the accusation of "you, you, you" out of the conversation and replacing it with ownership: "me, me, me."

The idea is to bring the problem to the forefront but expressing how it makes you feel and why you feel that way while offering a possible solution.

It can be easy to start using phrases, such as "you always do this," or "you never do this," and blame the other person. It only creates defensive walls and often escalates the situation.

The real key to using the "dialogue script" is to offer a solution —not to create a negative spiral or another argument.

The solution may not be finite or absolute, but at least the door will open for possibilities and not missed opportunities due to using the "you, you, you" approach.

SIMPLIFYING YOUR LIFE

EXERCISE #3 (FROM CHAPTER 7)

Step #1. Do a brain dump.

A brain dump is taking all those thoughts in your head—the good and the bad—and releasing them. Everything that is stressing you out, pissing you off, or making you feel over-whelmed—write it all down.

What's on your to-do list? What are you avoiding? What's something you need to get out of your head? Oftentimes when I do this, I have four or five handwritten pages filled with all the clutter that's been crowding my mind. Now, it's all laid out in rows on paper instead of jumbled in my mind.

Step #2. Find your number one stressor in this moment.

Take your brain dump and underline your top 10 stressors. Next, circle your top three, then place a star by the number one thing that is stressing you out.

Most people get overwhelmed at this part. It can be scary walking through the whole process. Give yourself permission to feel what you need to as you work through this process.

Step #3. Look at that top stressor on your list and ask yourself the following four questions:

1. How can I look at this stressor differently?
2. What's a possible solution to this stressor?
3. Am I willing to address this today?
4. What's one thing that I can do right now to begin to clear this?

Remember, the goal is to take control of your space, time, and energy.

THE CLARITY EXERCISE

EXERCISE #4 (FROM CHAPTER 10)

1. What is My Intention?

Intention starts with an objective. If you want to be healthier, what does that look like in smaller steps? It could be incorporating more fruit and vegetables in your diet, working out 30 minutes a day, or joining a fitness class.

By identifying your intention, you can create smaller steps toward reaching your objective.

2. What Obstacles May be in My Way?

What obstacles are keeping you from reaching your goal? Your busy schedule? Continually hitting snooze and waking up later? Constant low energy from stress?

Take a moment to write down your objective, intention, and everything that is keeping you from attainment. Once you've discovered these, it's time to plan how to break old habits and form positive, new ones. Start your day with your intention rather than creating excuses for yourself.

Think about the ways you can reach your objective every single day. Whether it's grocery shopping for different foods rather than getting fast food or taking 30 minutes before work to exercise, you have to correlate your intention to your action.

Remember, it only takes a very small shift in your day to make a big impact.

CREATING YOUR DREAM LIFE

EXERCISE #5 (FROM CHAPTER 11)

This exercise can help you begin to establish true vision for your life.

Question #1: What is my current reality? Where am I at right now? What does my life look like, feel like, etc.

Don't censor yourself or write for anybody else. This is for you. Pull your notebook out again and free-write every- thing that feels hard, what comes easy, and what is good or bad in your current reality. Let it flow.

Question #2: How do I feel about where I'm at? Why do I feel this way?

The more honest you can be here, the closer you are to reaching your true vision. Find the cracks you often fall into, what holds you back, and what interactions make you feel a particular way. This can relate to your personal life, relation- ships, or work—whatever is affecting you at this moment. Be as specific as possible.

Question #3: What is My Dream Life? If I could have anything in the world, what would it be? How would My life look?

Be specific! Include everything from the type of people you want to hang around to your occupation, to the foods you eat, to your daily routine.

I recommend that you take your time on this exercise and consider devoting an entire page to each aspect of your life: work, health, friends, house, etc.

The more you can sit with your thoughts and your vision for the future, the more accessible this future becomes.

LIVING A LIFE OF EASE & OPPORTUNITY

EXERCISE #6 (FROM CHAPTER 11)

Deep down, we all want to live a life that exudes ease. Many grow up with the mentality that we have to "work hard" to get what we want in life.

But what if there was an easier way?

What if life didn't have to be so hard?

What blocks most people in this part is the issue of defining clearly what feels easy and aligned for them. What comes easy for one person isn't necessarily easy for someone else.

Let's try to define what this looks like. To help with this answer the following questions:

1. What does "Ease" look like for me?
2. Have I ever experienced ease and flow? If yes, when?
3. Who do I know that lives a life of Ease?
4. What are those people doing differently than me?

5. What can I learn from those who live and manifest with ease and flow?

These people don't just trust in what they want in life, they believe without a doubt that they will receive it.

They know that the Universe will provide for their desires.

They don't hope or wait—they believe!

When you desire something, know that you are more than ready to receive it. Begin to envision yourself living a life of Ease and Flow! Begin to Embody those feelings daily.

10 X 10 X 10 EXERCISE

EXERCISE #7 (FROM CHAPTER 13)

This is something that can be done daily or weekly as a practice, or simply anytime you need a 1° Shift.

1. Write down 10 things for which you are grateful.
2. Then, write down 10 things you appreciate.
3. Write the 10 things you're manifesting and focus on how excited you would feel to have these things in your life.

I like to write each one back to back.

For Example:

"I am so grateful and thankful for my car."

"I appreciate that it always gets me where I need to go."

"I am so excited that my new car will be even more reliable and fuel-efficient."

"I am so grateful and thankful for the education that I have."

"I appreciate that it helps me to do my job well."

"I am so excited that this education opens up massive doors for me."

"I am so grateful and thankful for the connection that I have with my kids."

"I appreciate that we can have candid conversations with open honesty."

"I am so excited for the impact they are making on the world."

When you do this, you are not only activating the "Law of Thinking" and the "Law of Increase," but you are also bringing in the magnetic aspects of the "Law of Attraction." You become an energetic match for the desires in your heart.

Whenever you feel down or insecure, take a moment to apply the 10 x 10 x 10 exercise to experience a massive shift in energy.

THE 1° SHIFT METHOD SIMPLIFIED

EXERCISE #8 (FROM CHAPTER 16)

Step #1. What is the situation? Fact + Feeling

Where in your life are you looking for change? How does this situation make you feel? What is _actually_ going on in this area?

Step #2. What do I want instead?

Pause for a moment and imagine the burdens that you've experienced being lifted. How would that feel?

Step #3. Am I willing to do something about the issue?

For a shift to exist, you must be aware of your willingness to shift.

Step #4. What is the opportunity hidden inside the obstacle?

What opportunities can you see in the situation in front of you?

Step #5. What is one small step I can take right now?

What is one tiny action you can take today?

Step #6. Commit to taking action.

When you commit to taking action a world of possibilities opens up to you.

Step #7. Look for the evidence of it working—the result.

Consider what it looks like to pop one kernel of popcorn every day. You won't see the evidence of progress at first, but over time, you'll have a full bowl of popcorn! The same goes for that 1° Shift in your life.

After a while, results will begin to reveal themselves.

Each little shift helps you break out of old habits and form new, healthier ones that put you on the path toward changing your life.

The process will gradually become easier and more natural as you progress. It's happened to me, my kids, and every client with whom I work. Change is possible

SHARE THE SHIFT

If you loved this book, I ask that you do three things to keep this movement growing.

1. Write a review on Amazon as well as Barnes & Noble.
2. Connect with our community by using the hashtag #1DegreeShift on social media.
3. Give copies of this book to everyone you think will love it!

Sharing how this book has impacted you will create a ripple effect that will positively impact millions of lives 1° at a time!

For Bulk Orders Contact: Support@FloraSage.com.

Let's stay connected!
Website: www.florasage.com
Facebook: www.facebook.com/FloraSage
YouTube: www.youtube.com/c/FloraSage
LinkedIn: www.linkedin.com/in/flora-sage
Instagram: @florasageofficial

Ingram Content Group UK Ltd.
Milton Keynes UK
UKHW010802270323
419227UK00004B/479

9 781735 750309